Building
for Hope

MARWA AL-SABOUNI

Building for Hope

Towards an Architecture of Belonging

With 24 illustrations

CONTENTS

Preface p. 9

Introduction p. 12

1 p. 19
THE FEAR OF DEATH
Attaining Continuity

In which the author considers the human instinct for self-preservation, and how modernity's disconnection from the past undermines our sense of home; explores the ideas of character, dignity and continuity in architecture; and reflects on the challenges facing the reconstruction project in Syria.

2 p. 51
THE FEAR OF NEED
The Search for Abundance

In which the author introduces the concept of Factory Syndrome, which has undermined the social fabric of communities around the world; describes Ibn Khaldoun's ideas of 'umran and 'asabiyya; and explains how the quality of generosity can be expressed through architecture, helping cities to thrive.

3 p. 91
THE FEAR OF TREACHERY
Finding the Exit

In which the author examines the role of boundaries in architecture, drawing on urban theory as well as elements of traditional Islamic design and culture; looks at life in various cities through the prism of these ideas; gives an account of socio-economic change in Damascus during the late Ottoman period; and addresses 20th-century shifts in the relationship between rural and urban communities.

4   p. 131
THE FEAR OF LONELINESS
Achieving Acceptance

   In which the author considers the rural–urban binary in various
   contexts, including the Garden City movement and the Tanzimat
   land reforms; details the human impact of modern developments
   in Syrian property law; and emphasizes the importance of a local
   craft economy in combating isolation and allowing communities
   to flourish.

5   p. 167
THE FEAR OF BOREDOM
The Kaleidoscope of Meaning

   In which the author describes the effects of inequality, conflict
   and colonization on Syria's built environment; explores shifts in
   cultural meaning through the story of two Damascene libraries and
   a broader discussion of the city's dual identity; considers the effects
   of the Factory system on the work of architects, drawing on Finnish
   architectural history as a representative narrative; and offers her
   views on how to build in a way that supports ʿumran.

Notes **p. 211**

Acknowledgments **p. 218**

Index **p. 220**

PREFACE

After I wrote *The Battle for Home*, my book about the ways in which poor architecture has contributed to the conflict in my country, people frequently asked me to propose a plan for building our way out of the mess: *Describe your dream city, describe your dream home.* I looked up my sleeve for the model they were expecting me to pull out, but found no such thing – only more questions.

I have come to understand that the ruin of home is not necessarily expressed in the rubble scattered in what was once a street: it can also be seen in shattered societies, empty lives or an ongoing conflict that has lost its way. It is true that war leaves behind wounded cities, or even dead cities, but I discovered that our world is also blighted by many sick cities, the cries of which are no less urgent than the cries of those devastated by war.

What is your dream home? In a destroyed country like Syria, many no longer dare to ask such a question, because the road to dreams is filled with rubble. So people tend to take a different route, focusing on far-away destinations where the future still lives. They leave behind the question of the dream home, expecting architects like myself to seek opportunity in the aftermath of tragedy, to make a wearable dress from the torn rags of war.

Describe Utopia, describe your dream home: the request is repeated again and again. But I do not wish to start from there. I do not wish to imagine a Utopia because I do not believe in cities that float up in our dreams, to be built on blank pages, *tabula rasa* like those of the bombed cities of the Second World War or those destroyed in the current Syrian conflict. For underneath the rubble, there is still a context: even without a neighbourhood, there is still a past. The traces of memories and experiences remain. And in the absence of building there will still be space, soil, air, weather and orientation.

We cannot imagine our dream home without engaging with reality: we must ask ourselves, of which materials should it be built, what kind of stone, wood or mortar? We cannot begin to design it without imagining its location and picturing its surroundings. It cannot just drift onto any coast, or land on any street. For every place has a colour, a smell and a texture. It has a humidity and a temperature. Every land has its own sky, and every window its own breeze.

Dream homes and dream cities remain in dreams. They have no inhabitants and no societies. Yet many of today's cities were born of modernist dreams in the wake of war or rapid economic change. Dubai, Tokyo and Rotterdam are examples of such cities: built on the pillars of clouds, with no foundations.

For some people who realize these truths, the answer is to shut the doors of the imagination: to seat architects on the side benches and open-source architecture to the public so that they can build their dream homes, house by house and street by street. But again I find myself at odds with this approach, because our cities and homes cannot be an accumulation of random sectors. They should reflect an underlying logic and exist in harmony with one another – just as an orchard is held together by its roots, but also divided into sections and wisely planned, allowing high trees and lower plants to thrive in balance.

So what is the answer? How do we rebuild our destroyed cities and regain our abandoned homes? If a ready-made solution is rejected and a patchwork one is not enough, is there an answer to this dilemma?

Perhaps it lies in rephrasing the question to ask not how our cities should look, but rather, how they should make us feel. Instead of searching for the image first in order to beget the feeling, perhaps we need to identify the feeling before the right image can be found.

In this book, I therefore start by exploring a set of emotions that set traps for the practice of architecture. The book begins with an exploration of the distinction between the colonizers and the colonized, but it goes on to address the merging of settlement patterns as a result of the globalizing forces that are dissolving all boundaries.

In Arabic, the verb *yaskun* refers to dwelling. It is related to the term *sukun*, which means stillness, in the sense of locational and psychological stability. To find a place that does not push us to leave it behind and move away from it, a place for our souls and selves to dwell – *taskun* – that surely is the task our world now demands of us, and architecture plays no small part in it.

Just as building can lead to conflict, it can help to bring about peace. We build for peace when we understand what this delicate act involves. As well as bricks and mortar, it means incorporating our deepest fears – and our utmost hopes – not only into what we build, but into how it is done.

INTRODUCTION

Ever since civil war broke out in my country, I have been asking myself what lies beneath the upsurge of violence, division, frustration and despair that has taken place. Over the past few years I have been fortunate enough to travel to parts of the world I had never visited before, meeting new people and engaging in lively discussion. It has been fascinating but also troubling to see that the social and urban transformations which ignited war and bloodshed in my country are spreading around the world. Each time I return, I carry a stronger conviction that we share much more than we know – and certainly more than we care to admit.

When I meet people in Europe, I am often asked how I feel in the face of European prosperity and grandeur, coming as I do from a place like Syria that they perceive as destroyed and in pieces. I'm always perplexed by this question, because I see neither prosperity nor grandeur in Europe. What I do see frightens me and makes my heart sink, because it looks like the other side of the mirror – it looks like the future that awaits us in the reconstruction of Syria, which seems as dark as war.

It is not only flesh and blood that we all have in common, but history too. Our historical narratives may vary, but they share trajectories, cusps and consequences. The stories of conquerors and the conquered; the traps set for societies prior to war and the chains wrapped around their necks in the aftermath; the light of faith, love and solidarity, the darkness of lies and deception; the experience of fear and violence, the loss of certainty, the loss of home – all these we share.

However, recent history is marked with a sharp division that forms one part of the subject matter of this book: the division between the colonizers and the colonized, the defeated and the victorious. For a long time, triumphant colonial powers dictated the rules of the game, but now the natural consequences of their actions are spreading beyond containment. The colonialism that created empires and left behind hellholes has led of its own accord to globalization. The same structures that were eroded in defeated colonies are now collapsing in the home territories of former colonial powers, swept away by global forces that no one knows how to contain.

Our problems around the world are no longer separate; the soaring pillars of the world's roof are being gnawed away at the base. We collectively stare in confusion, denial and fear at the looming crises in food, water and clean air, while the problems of migration, division, unrest and crime unsettle all of us. The word 'rights' is uttered countless times each day, yet rights are violated on all sides and there is no clear agreement as to how to define them. In an era that dares to call itself progressive, we have no clear conception of the things that cannot be done.

This book chooses a different way to speak of rights and to look at the places and possessors of power. Instead of focusing on human influence and entitlement, it examines the vulnerabilities that we humans share. Our story was painted on the walls of the prehistoric caves where we first took refuge from wild beasts and storms; today, it is still represented by the marks we leave on the earth, the places we build for our protection and where we settle side by side. This book looks at how we relate to our built environment; at what we tell it and what it tells us; at when we can call it *home*.

In *The Battle for Home*, I addressed the question 'Why do we need home?' In this book, the question revolves around the 'how'. How is home built, and what does it mean to us emotionally? We in Syria have lost our home, and the project of rebuilding looms over us like a black cloud. It doesn't take much insight to see how much of our world has been destroyed of late, nor how the process of repairing that damage may end up rewarding the very people who caused it. That is not the only worry; there is also the problem of the way in which we build. Often it seems that when we restore somewhere, we create a nowhere.

In pursuing this quest to understand the 'how' of human settlement, I have encountered many stories: stories of money, history, ethics and, regrettably, more wars. There is a tendency in mainstream approaches to the subject of settlement (even when they are interdisciplinary) to discuss problems and their symptoms while overlooking the causes. I hope that the stories and disciplines I have tried to weave together here will shed some much-needed light on those underlying causes.

Because the topic of settlement is so intricate and extensive, I have attempted to consider it in terms of a few basic categories: nomadic, rural and urban settlement, as well as what lies in between. Through these categories I tell the story of building in different parts of the world, but my focus remains on Syria. This is not only because it is my country and the place where I have always lived, but because it is the oldest place of settlement in the world – the place where human civilization is supposed to have sprung up, and where the traders of the ancient world met at a crossroads.

I choose to look at the stories here through the glass of human vulnerability, the most naked and essential part of our being. It is the part we cannot avoid and from which we have no choice but to learn. In the course of our journey through life, we can strive either to suppress this vulnerability or to call a greater power – a transcendent power – to our aid. The decision to confront one's own vulnerability is an ethical choice, the acceptance of a moral obligation to both self and others. We are constantly seeking a balance between that which reminds us of our weakness and that which brings strength through hope.

Our buildings and the way we relate to them are an important part of this quest. They hold the key to something hidden deep within us, something this book tries to define. Our collective memory returns always to that oneiric cave, and our species memory of the safety it provided guides us in our understanding of how to build 'home'. All the threads of human settlement meet at the crossroads of architecture; political and economic forces are embodied in our buildings, and they can be both advanced and held back by architectural forms.

Thinking about all of this, I came to the conclusion that there are five principal fears which comprise our sense of vulnerability as humans. These fears, I believe, are an essential element in how we address the question of belonging.

The fear of death is the most radical of the five: it is in our nature to seek protection from life-threatening dangers. But the avoidance of physical harm is only part of this fear, since what underlies our attachment to life is a desire that is more metaphysical than physical: a desire for *more time*, time that could stretch to eternity, granting us immortality. Rationally we know that this desire is unattainable; yet our fear of the diminishing returns of real time springs from our consciousness of our own mortality, while our desire for endless survival belongs to an unconscious sense of our human superiority in an atrophied universe.

When our immediate survival is secured, other fears come to the fore. We are haunted by questions about how to earn a living, how much things cost and so on. This can be summarized as a fear of need – closely connected to the fear of death, but distinct from it. The desire to have *more* does not revolve around time, but around power: power over what surrounds us.

With abundance comes competition, and with it the fear of treachery. Our inner world becomes dominated by suspicion of anyone around us who might be a source of harm. This in turn leads to the fear of loneliness, of having no one on whom to depend or in whom to put our trust. Finally, when we have overcome these challenges and surrounded ourselves with security, abundance and acceptance, we find ourselves facing the fear of boredom – the fear that our hard-won survival might mean nothing after all, and our achievements will count for nothing in our inevitable meeting with death. And so we are returned to the fear from which this circular journey began.

The only way to manage these fears is to find meaning, and one way of doing this is through the buildings that surround us and create our shared sense of home. In the past, we have built our way towards meaning in our homes and markets, our orchards and religious buildings – and I hope to show how, in the future, we might do so again. My argument is not merely aesthetic, but weaves in elements of politics and economics. I consider the five fears in relation to the built environment in order to better understand how we might make our cities, our villages and our world into safer places, places where we belong.

Although the main subject of the book is reconstruction in the aftermath of war, it is not relevant only to destroyed cities. Cities that stand intact can also rearrange themselves, whether to help their inhabitants settle or to unsettle them; and the loss of home, of a sense of belonging, is something from which many places suffer today. I want to explore the qualities that a place can possess in order to help people settle there and attain that feeling of belonging.

This process of settlement and belonging, involving the two poles of people and place, is a continuous cycle: we cannot determine its starting point, whether it begins with the human or with the place. Each reciprocally affects the other. People create meaning in a place, but place offers channels and anchors to human behaviour – as well as obstacles and cliffs on which the cycle might break.

Nonetheless, there are two important points to bear in mind. The first is that the qualities of a place are inescapably related to its natural features; they are the source of its character. Humans are responsible for staying true to that character in the way that they develop settlements. All the great settlements we admire are outgrowths of the natural order that preceded them: Paris grew from the Seine and its islands, Rome from the Tiber and its seven hills – and, as we will see in this book, Damascus from the river Barada, Mount Qasioun and the Ghouta.

The second point is that humans mostly live collectively, so if there is to be an established and durable form of settlement with an associated sense of belonging, a distinction must be made between individual and collective interest in its design. Belonging is an individual condition, whereas settlement is collective; yet they are interrelated and interdependent.

My intention is to frame the five fears in relation to place so that they do not remain mere effects without causes. If I wrote about the five fears strictly from the human perspective, the result would be a study of feelings and emotions – a psychoanalytical work, describing the inner micro-world of human nature and how this affects what we perceive and experience. But it would lack a comprehensive vision of how to master these emotions – something that is vital, in my perspective, to understanding the cycle whereby we humans come to be at home.

The urban world and its economic, political and social matrices, on which I have tried to focus, are inseparable from the architectural world, from its aesthetic qualities and the psychological and moral relationships that they inspire.

In his poem 'This is Damascus', the Syrian poet Nizar Qabbani writes: 'Here are my roots. Here is my heart. Here is my language. So how can I make my love for my homeland clear? Is there clarification in love?!'

In my view, roots, heart and language do serve to clarify our sense of home – but how? This book may shed some light on that question.

Homs

5 January 2019

1 THE FEAR OF DEATH
Attaining Continuity

In reaction to the German Blitz on London during the Second World War, Churchill's friend and advisor Professor Frederick Lindemann – aka 'the Prof' – sent the prime minister a memorandum that subsequently became known as the Dehousing Paper. It proposed that German cities like Hamburg and Dresden should be reduced to rubble, stating that 'having one's home demolished is most damaging to morale. People seem to mind it more than having their friends or even relatives killed....There seems little doubt that this would break the spirit of the people.'[1]

Effective it certainly was, as it reshaped the way 'victory' could be achieved in modern warfare. Now, decades after the destruction of Nagasaki and Cologne, the world is watching a new list of cities that have been subjected to mass destruction. Images of this devastation have been captured by drones hovering over the part of the world called the Middle East, where the death of civilization and humanity itself can be read in crumbling cement and the dust of crushed breeze blocks.

Some are tempted to term the chaos and turmoil in the Middle East a third world war, owing to the complexity of interests at stake and the number of 'players' on the ground; yet the enemy is no outsider. Unlike the previous two world wars – and despite all the foreign forces involved – in most cases, the destruction is being caused by the very people who reside in the place. This phenomenon is not peculiar to one region. It has become so pervasive that it has a name: urban warfare. At international peace platforms around the world, experts grapple with the problem of containing the flames of internal struggle in places where wars are no longer launched from a chamber of high command, but rather from the basement next door.

The mainstream explanation is that the forces of technology and globalization have fallen into the wrong hands, creating the conditions for urban and guerilla warfare. But as historian Peter Frankopan argues in his book *The Silk Roads*, neither technology nor globalization are products of our time; in fact, the ancient world was just as affected by immigration and free trade as ours today. 'We think of globalization as a uniquely modern phenomenon,' he writes, 'yet 2,000 years ago too, it was a fact of life, one that presented opportunities, created problems and promoted technological advance.'[2]

While many parts of the world are still fortunate enough not to be occupied by endless wars, the divisions that are evident within so many societies make it clear that the distance between zones of peace and conflict is narrowing at an alarming pace. Even if peaceful places are not yet erupting in mass violence, their disunity means they can no longer truly call themselves secure.

So we must ask ourselves: what is the reason behind the world's internal fragility? Has it always been like this, or is it a modern phenomenon? Historical accounts such as Frankopan's may lead us to conclude that not much has changed, and there are plausible reasons for believing this. Our ancestors wanted the same as we do now – namely a 'good life' – so they traded, travelled and expanded. Their sense of competition allowed them to build great nations and to fight wars. If we read history like this, we might not see many radical changes between their times and ours.

But on a closer examination of today's world, other aspects become more noticeable. Never before in history have people been so inclined to detach themselves from their places, lands and houses, or so confused about defining their home. The policy announced in the Dehousing Paper of 1942 might not be as effective today, for in many parts of the world the experience of home is now radically compromised. There are increasing numbers of rough sleepers even in the most developed cities, and the seemingly endless flux of refugees adds to our sense of displacement. More importantly, many people have lost touch with the very concept of home, experiencing homelessness despite having the modern luxury of a roof over their heads. Home is more than a house, and in some cases less than a house – it is a place of belonging.

When 'the Prof' advised Churchill to focus his raids on people's houses, his aim was to break the morale of the enemy by creating fear. It is not only the love we have for our homes that has traditionally made us grieve at their disappearance; it is also the fear of what it would mean to lose them. Whether on the larger scale of lands, cities, towns, neighbourhoods and streets or at the more modest level of houses, flats and sheds, our homes have always had the ability to make us feel safe – not merely in the immediate sense of providing shelter that protects us from the hazards and inconveniences outside, but in the deeper sense of being secure and settled where we belong. The question is, why has modern humanity apparently abandoned this attachment to home? Why are we now so ambivalent about settling down?

I do not think we humans have really changed our position concerning what roots us in our surroundings. Instead, what has changed is that these surroundings have become alien to us. One of the most highly developed arts of our modern age is that of manipulating appearances: changing the surface, rather than the substance beneath. Nonetheless, sometimes even a surface change can hit us at the core of our being. A change in the way things appear can produce a profound instability in the way things are.

Ancient civilizations have passed down countless innovations to ours. Whether it is what we have read in the pages of Greek philosophy, or in Hammurabi's laws; adopted from the Sasanian bureaucracy or the Roman artillery; taken from Chinese culture, which introduced the world to paper, ink, powder, silk and even football; applied according to the chemistry and astronomy of the pharaohs; derived from the 10th-century Muslims' introduction of the zero, logarithms, the minor blood cycle and world mapping – it makes no fundamental difference whether we print these discoveries out on A4 paper or read them from a vellum scroll. The discoveries have been made, and they endure.

Indeed, if we could strip away the technological advances of the modern age – which, despite their importance, have primarily affected our experience of speed and distance, how far we go and how long it takes – we might notice that we have made surprisingly few real breakthroughs. We might characterize the life we call 'modern' as a continuation of long-familiar habits and ancient competencies. Nonetheless, when it comes to building, we are faced with a real break in continuity between our time and earlier periods of history.

In all major civilizations of the past, different styles of architecture were created, a range of building techniques were used, various heights and forms were established as typical; but the basic building materials remained the same. Now, however, for the first time in history, man is producing hybrid and synthetic materials, and in the large quantities made possible by industrialization and automation. Mass production followed by robotization is saturating the building market, dictating the scale of our products and the way in which we build. The consequences of this exceed the immediate disconnection between form and function. A more critical disconnection is being brought about between human beings and their sense of place.

In principle, the instinct for self-preservation equates to a fear of death. Throughout history, humankind has always been haunted by this fear, seeking to postpone our inevitable destiny. We hear about such ambitions in the fields of science and medicine: a never-ending quest to develop the fountain of eternal youth in a pill. Yet what could be more threatening than eternity if it contains pain and danger? Our minds can cope with the torment of pain, illness and fear if they're temporary, but when attached to the idea of eternity they become unbearable. On the other hand, pleasures such as love, happiness, and wealth cease to please once we realize their ephemeral nature.

The condition of enjoyment is its continuation, but no such thing is possible on earth. When we encounter pain for a period of time our minds imagine eternal misery, and when we encounter pleasure our minds instantly fear that it will soon come to an end. To the 18th-century philosopher Edmund Burke, in his *Philosophical Enquiry into the Origin of Our Ideas of the Sublime and Beautiful*, 'the ideas of eternity, and infinity, are among the most affecting we have, and yet perhaps there is nothing of which we really understand so little, as of infinity and eternity'.[3] But I believe these concepts can help to explain many of our material preferences and architectural judgments.

In a series of articles written in 1928, the American architect Frank Lloyd Wright discusses modern architecture through the prism of building materials. He concludes that 'perhaps the greatest difference eventually between ancient and modern buildings will be due to our modern machine-made glass. Glass in any wide utilitarian sense, is new.'[4] In this article Wright makes several assertions: he states that had the ancients been able to use glass in their buildings, as we can do with the help of our modern machines, 'the history of architecture would have been radically different'; furthermore, he sees that glass, which he calls ' the curse of the classic', has not been fully embraced by architects, who are being shackled by 'traditional ideas of what a building must look like' – so he urges them to join him in fully embracing glass 'as a crystal' with which to build cities 'iridescent by day, luminous by night, imperishable' in which the use of light will replace the need for shadow.[5]

In his dream of a crystal city, Wright was envisioning the creation of an 'imperishable' place, a place like no other, one that would break from what buildings 'must look like'. By being original, it could be immortal. But to what extent is this true?

Revisiting Burke's *Enquiry* sheds some light on this. Burke distinguished objects in terms of the sublime and the beautiful, according to the impressions they leave on us. The beautiful is whatever excites pleasure, whereas the sublime is whatever excites delight. To Burke, a high mountain, a vast valley, a dark temple interior or a written passage imbued with obscurity were all sublime objects. To set yourself against a mountain is to imagine your own size, your ability to cross, to climb, even to surround it in sight. Naturally you feel dwarfed by the mountain; you sense the limits of your capability to engage with it, and in order to come to this realization you imagine the pain in your legs, the slips and the falls, the tension in your muscles, the fact that you are spared the reality of this pain – and this makes you feel delighted.

According to Burke, the eye experiences a kind of physical pain or tension in the retina and its muscles while trying to capture the full dimensions and details of a great object. This parallels the psychological tension of self-projection in comparison with or defiance of the sublime – although such emotions should not threaten us to the same degree as an imminent danger – and the relief from the combined sensations is, again, a source of delight.

Wright's plea on behalf of glass was revolutionary, driven by an architect's urge for bold experimentation with a rich legacy of sensitive exploration of form and material. However, I doubt he would consider his dream to have been fulfilled by today's modern city of glass. For the glass box has proved to be neither sublime nor beautiful: in fact, it makes a weak impression on the mind. Not only does its transparent surface have no expression, but its fragility holds no promise that it will *last*.

It may not be possible to live forever, but objects and structures can outlive their makers and owners, carrying their names forever.

It doesn't have to be the palace of a ruler that grants such a privilege. If your family home has endured shelling and earthquakes along with wind and rain, it deserves recognition and respect as the continuing representation of a life, an extension of a continuing existence: *yours*.

The dehousing proposed by Lindemann in the early 20th century was effective primarily because it eradicated its victims' existence. The current 'urban war' in the Middle East does the same thing, with one major difference: for many today, 'home' has ceased to exist long before its final destruction. Our homes lose their associations and continuity is broken even before they are bombed into rubble.

In spiritual traditions, continuity is linked to divinity – the Creator is the only everlasting truth, and it is by referring all universal matters to the divine that continuity is possible. But such a belief doesn't necessarily satisfy the human longing for other, more tangible forms of continuity. By surrounding ourselves in our built environment with elements of the created universe – the mountains' stones, the land's wood and soil – we remind ourselves of nature's permanence and our affinity with it.

At the other end of the spectrum lies the materialistic human urge to take control of what intimidates us, to dominate the natural world by creating counterparts to it. Here we are reminded of the historical attempts of rulers to immortalize their own names by building 'sublime' objects designed to perpetuate their own existence. This has given rise to structures like the pyramids, or Burj Khalifa, that arrogantly soaring tower in the centre of Dubai. Still, because they are built in stone, the pyramids appeal to us in something like the way mountains do; whereas Burj Khalifa, seeking to bring the sky to its knees, is in conflict with every atom of our nature.

Buildings can provide us with a sublime sense of permanence, but they can also be unsettling for that very reason. Some of the greatest buildings in history were built to intimidate or to create a sense of unease; we might rejoice in or take delight in them for a moment, but we would not wish to live in them. The significance of such buildings as works of architecture is that they are a collective accomplishment in which we take pride, as for example the French do in the Eiffel Tower, or New Yorkers in the Empire State Building. They are cherished for the structural excellence that qualifies them as sublime, and for their solidity, which confers continuity; and they achieve these qualities without stepping over the line in the manner of Burj Khalifa. Such buildings move us in much the same way as sheer cliffs and thundering waterfalls – providing we take them in small doses.

In short, we take pride in the sublime, but we settle around the beautiful. The fault of our modern architecture is that it has, with very few exceptions, failed to achieve this balance. Modern architecture was the child of war. It was an outcome of the need to reconstruct swathes of destroyed cities, and also to use the products of a new age. Building was undertaken to impress, to house, to experiment – but building to last was not part of the deal.

Pinning down what is really valued in old buildings and artefacts has occupied the minds of many scholars and philosophers, whose works offer thought-provoking explanations. Some of them have also been busy theorizing what has *not* been valuable in modern buildings. What may be more useful now is a focus on trying to find a bridge between the past and the future.

Every new civilization brings a leap forward in certain fields of knowledge. Whether this leap takes place in science, technology, culture, literature or philosophy, it is typically accompanied by a surge in production and an enhancement of quality, an increase in wealth and, in most cases, an expansion of territory. Intellectual progress is reflected in new buildings, the opening of new roads, the development of infrastructure and so on. How is any of this different from modernity, which today seems to be blamed – justly or not – for all the world's woes? Why does the disconnection between past and present now seem so much more abrupt than at any other time in history? A divorce, rather than the usual historic dialogue – such is what we observe between what we now call our 'heritage' and our present. Much contemporary architecture no longer aspires to express the zeitgeist; instead, it is constantly aiming at the future. The more 'futuristic' a building, the more successful it is thought to be. Is this an indication that our current time has no real value in itself? Is the carrot of 'the future' dangled in order to divert attention from a present-day void?

Since all those who have tried (and are still trying) to answer these questions belong either to the past or the present, I thought a new voice 'from the future' might provide fresh insight. I looked no further than my own living room, turning to my fifteen-year-old daughter. Her age places her in default opposition to whatever I have to say – which was exactly what I needed.

When I wrote *The Battle for Home*, my daughter thought it was absolutely ridiculous to suggest that architecture could be a factor leading to war. She was a child of war herself, having been only six years old when Homs ignited in 2011. She gave up a precious part of her childhood to wartime fear and deprivation, and while growing up in those unusual circumstances she became aware of many differences between her generation of Syrian children and their peers around the world.

When she hears me speak passionately about our traditional architecture in Syria and the legacy of the Islamic old city, she turns into an even stauncher advocate of modernity and its conveniences. For her, Dubai and its shiny towers and mega shopping malls represent the ideal our collapsing cities must strive to live up to, especially now in the rebuilding process. 'We have to catch up with the spirit of the age,' she warns me.

My daughter insists that she is not merely speaking as a millennial – she is not opposing me for the sake of opposition, or echoing stereotypes fed to her by the media (to list a few of the charges her mother may accuse her of). Her perspective is based on a reality she experiences every day – unlike mine, which is rooted in a fading past. Indeed, she represents a wide spectrum of people, not only in Syria but around the world, who believe that calls like my own for a conceptual retreat from modernity suffer from hopeless weakness and sentimental nostalgia that has no place in the practicality of our modern world.

But I know that my doubts about modernity have nothing to do with nostalgia. They are related to concern about the mysterious disconnection I believe it has caused. I also know that when it comes to architecture, my daughter has only caught a glimpse of what 'modern' actually means, and that the term has acquired – especially over the last few decades – a polyvalent character, encompassing trends of sustainability, nature-mimicry, context-conscious architecture and so on. Nonetheless, in my view, despite their benign premises these trends still share an imponderable quality that keeps them jigsawed with modernity at the very disconnection I'm having a problem with.

All I need to do is to focus the conversation between me and my daughter on this. Easier said than done!

Starting from the basics, I ask her: what is modernity? Can you boil it down to its essence? In response, she says: 'The least amount of effort put in, with the most amount of time to gain.'

The answer impresses me; in a sense, I think it is indeed the essence of modernity. But I'm not ready to be defeated at the first blow. I persevere: 'But don't you see an imbalance in this deal? More time for less work?'

'Here we go!' my daughter exclaims, anticipating one of my 'moral sermons'.

She may be right in her reaction, as I was just about to explain to her what lies behind the mask of this excess of time and saved effort: how nature doesn't like a void, how the deal of modernity she describes has led to excessive production. How this unnecessary increase has led to various patterns of imbalance that have manifested themselves in building – building bigger and taller, enlarging scales, travelling longer and further. With all of this has come a deeper inequality, sharper differences in social classes, fiercer social competition; not to mention multi-level living in stacked boxes and, at the other end of the spectrum, a mushrooming of slums.

Social breakdown is, without a doubt, the illness of this age we call modern. It is a prime underlying factor in the war in Syria, just as it is in the creation of the so-called 'suicide belt' in the western United States – where, according to the Princeton academic Angus Deaton, people literally kill themselves over a 'failure in spiritual and social life'.[6] Such failure is almost inevitable where cities are built to divide people rather than to bring us together.

Teachers around the world complain that they feel as if they are walking on eggshells when they talk to millennial students, and that this generation of young people seems much more vulnerable than their predecessors. What has this to do with modernity? Well, observers suggest a number of reasons for this individual fragility. One of them is that children do not play in the street any more, which has led to a drastic change in the pattern of how they interact with others. This may sound like a social trend more related to technology and video gaming, but the truth is, gaming is only a symptom. The root cause is that our streets are no longer regarded as safe. Those same observers point out that in some parts of the world, there are now laws criminalizing parents who let children play unattended in the park or street. People are afraid of kidnapping, molestation, rape, murder – and so kids are getting lonelier, and more fragile. The price of modernity is that there is nothing in our cities that can protect them without leading to isolation. Isolation is literally jeopardizing the very lives we seek to protect.

That conversation between me and my daughter ended like every conversation between a mother and her teenage daughter:

with a big sigh and a 'You don't get me, Mom.' But some time later, when the topic of 'cities that divide' came up again, she had very specific descriptions of those:

'Big distances: the further apart people are, the less they communicate. Higher densities: the more people are packed together, the less they communicate too. And houses that look like space capsules, white and flattened with no corners; there one cannot make memories. You see, Mom, astronauts are not sent to make memories in space.'

I was delighted at the prospect that we might find some common ground on this topic. I told her with great enthusiasm, 'Wow, I think we're on the same page!' But she was quick to correct me: 'No – I don't want people to communicate! It's better that they don't. I just want a nice house where I can have memories.'

Although my daughter doesn't share my concerns about people losing touch with their surroundings and neighbours (I still hope that one day she might!), her 'space capsule' example actually helped me to understand the disconnection between modernity and the past. Whether it takes the form of luxurious, large-scale living areas defined by big spaces and sheer surfaces, or of slums and informal settlements with high densities and rough edges, the modern ideal is in essence no more than a space capsule with little room for memories. Reflecting on this, I was taken back to my own childhood memories of seeing spaceships on TV; I remembered cartoon images of a tower with a slum at its foot, where soldiers flew around in capsules.

As children growing up in the eighties and nineties, my generation had limited options for entertainment compared to today's young people, for whom everything is a touch of a screen away. Back in those days, Syrian national TV consisted of a single broadcasting company. On our small TV in the kitchen, my siblings and I, like all Syrian children of our time, used to watch the two available channels: one broadcasting in Arabic, the other in English.

They were simply called the First Channel and the Second. On the First, we children had an hour and a half of cartoons each day around 4:00 p.m. – a very convenient time, after we had already had lunch and done some homework.

Syria at the time was under an economic siege imposed by international sanctions. In reaction, Ba'athist policies had a clear goal: strengthening local production and creating a self-sufficient internal economy, which could survive despite what was often called 'international blackmail'. This produced positive results in certain areas such as the textile and food sectors, and the local economy did start to show some signs of recovery. However, when it came to culture, strict rules of monitoring and censorship were imposed. All across the Arabic-speaking countries, the publishing industry was taking its last breaths. Culture became a hostage in the hands of strict leftists, who had been conditioned by loyalty to the established authority of the Ba'ath party and were reacting to the rise of the Muslim Brotherhood.

In Syria, this meant a generation culturally shaped by those ninety minutes of cartoons. But it wasn't all bad. The selections with which we were presented combined a wide range of stories from all over the world, from reworkings of classical works of literature to traditional fairy tales. I might never have held a copy of Hans Christian Andersen's works in my hand, but their scenes, narratives and moral lessons remain engraved in my memory, since they shaped my first uncertain steps towards the world of culture.

Whoever was behind choosing the cartoons, dubbing them into eloquent Arabic and writing the emotional songs with which they were topped and tailed, it would not be an exaggeration to say that he or she watered Syrian childhood at a time of intellectual and artistic aridity. The stories were diverse and rich in content, from the West and the East, from the past and from the present; some were even from the future, where mobile phones were still in the realm of science fiction. In their month-long progress, these epic tales, which always ended with a hopeful message, passed through some extremely painful episodes. They presented real-life dramas that pulled the throat up to the tongue and left you in an agony of suspense until the dénouement. The protagonists usually went through a life-changing struggle, whether looking for a lost parent or rescuing the earth from an apocalyptic fate. *Les Misérables* and *Treasure Island* were the lightweight exceptions to the diet of despair on which we feasted in our childhood afternoons.

One of the most successful series was a story based on Alexander Key's novel *The Incredible Tide*, aimed at teenagers and written in the 1970s. The Japanese director Hayao Miyazaki produced it in 1978 as an animated television series entitled *Future Boy Conan*. This adaptation later appeared on Arabic TV screens, dubbed with charismatic Iraqi and Kuwaiti voices and retitled *Adnan and Lina* (the Arabic names of the boy and girl protagonists). Over the past thirty-seven years it has become a familiar work throughout the region, constantly reshown on Arabic-language channels. The action takes place in a post-apocalyptic world devastated by a third world war; the use of magnetic weapons has diverted the earth's polar axis from its original angle. As a result, life and peace have been wiped from the face of the earth. Only two places remain in functional order: one is 'the Tower', where military forces use the enslaved people living in the shanty houses beneath them to help in the collection of solar energy. The quest to acquire this new form of energy has been interrupted by the disappearance of the one man who has the scientific key to it, Dr Rami. The other surviving place is the 'Land of Hope', a small village where nature has miraculously managed to survive the calamities of the war and where the last remaining community is secretly thriving, out of sight of the Tower. Lina is Dr Rami's young granddaughter; Adnan is the boy who helps in her search for her grandfather. He rescues Lina repeatedly from the hands of the Tower's military forces, who seek to capture the scientist through his granddaughter.

Aside from its compelling qualities as a thriller, love story and moral prophecy, what makes this story so interesting to me now, as an adult and an architect, is the incredible tide – the natural catastrophe by which the story ends as a consequence of the abuse of the ecosphere. Ultimately, the tide swallows the evil Tower along with the miserable slum at its foot, while the small cottages and stone houses at the Land of Hope survive, and with them humanity. The earth's equilibrium, disrupted by the unwise and greedy actions taken at the chamber of command in the Tower, is represented *architecturally* in the brutal, detached and oppressive forms of tower block and miserable slum. Likewise, the town in the Land of Hope is an architectural representation of a possible reconciliation between nature and human settlement – between fellow humans. Those two architectural forms, the Tower/slum at one end and the fabric of interwoven houses at the other, epito-mize the contradictions of our world: apocalypse versus hope, greed versus courage, injustice versus dignity. Within every form there is a correspondence between the moral thought it embodies and the psychological feeling it arouses. That is clearly captured in a work of literature such as *The Incredible Tide*. It is intriguing to ask why a tower represents the blind ambition, selfishness and cruelty of a criminal gang – and why does the Land of Hope not have highways and a downtown area of steel and glass? Why does the picture of the only surviving community on earth represent a small town built in stone, at a human scale and with a warm sense of detail?

Today, the kind of apocalyptic imagery depicted in *The Incredible Tide* is painted all over cities like Iraq's Mosul and Syria's Aleppo. These are examples of devastated places where talk of reconstruc-tion has followed news of revolt, siege, shelling and mass migration. Yet now, in the aftermath of the war, its bitter arguments are replaced by more practical questions, the chief of which is 'Where to begin?' And this turns out to be a deep and complicated matter.

One might argue that such moments of aftermath have faced all devastated towns and cities around the world, following wars and disasters throughout history. This is partly true; however, two main differences are overlooked in such an observation: the absence in the Middle East of not only a widely accepted, 'winning' architectural style, but a winning power.

The new world that was created after the Second World War produced its own architecture, which was used to cement a new set of beliefs; industrialization, science and technology became the basic ideological building blocks. The brutality of modern architecture provoked some concerned voices to draw attention to the social role of architecture, but the roar of the building industry proved to be much louder. Many European cities as the world knows them today were shaped – or rather, reshaped – by those crucial moments, in ways that have been both praised and lamented.

But unlike European and Japanese cities in the 20th century, which raised themselves from the ruins by leaning on the newly born modernist architecture and all the supposed certainties of modern thinking, the cities of the Middle East, erased by 'creative chaos',[7] find themselves in a more puzzling situation. All around us, standing in the ruins of the past, we hear voices telling us that modernity is dead. And it is not only the lack of a prevailing or 'winning' architectural style that makes it such a puzzle how to build and where to begin. It is the lack of something more complicated: an actual winner in our conflicts. In the aftermath of the Sykes–Picot agreement and civil war, everybody is a loser; and the existence of winners is not in the interests of the big foreign powers.

Since the philosopher David Hume wrote his 'Essay on the Balance of Power' in 1752, European policy, and later its borders, have been effectively shaped by the principle of the balance of power. Although the concept as argued by Hume wasn't new (dating back to the Greeks), Britain, a devoted supporter of the balance of power idea since the days of Henry VIII, found itself in the aftermath of the Second World War fighting almost alone for what Hitler had deemed an 'out-of-date political idea'.[8] Churchill declared in 1946 that the 'old doctrine of power balance is unsound', thereby announcing the beginnings of a unipolar order that lasted far longer than all the predictions of the anti-power-balance realists. It is only now that the war in my country has forced me not to immediately skip over news channels (to the cartoon!) that I have heard about a new order: a bipolar world created in the very arena we are living in here, in Syria. However, as the historian Edward Mead Earle once observed, 'The balance of power may well land us all in the cemetery'[9] – and there is now general acceptance of the view that the conflicting international interests and proxy wars played out in the region have left the Middle East in a perilous situation.

So when it comes to rebuilding Syria, for example – one of the main fields on which those interests play out – the myriad of players makes it almost impossible to come up with a unified vision or agree on a way forward. The land is imbued with the powder of vengeance and feud, ready to explode at the slightest spark. This volatility has many reasons internal to Syria, of course, and I will explore these over the course of this book; but a significant factor is the way the region has been kept on burning coals ever since the Ottoman period, using the same principles of power balance that the US and Europe abandoned decades ago.

The external support that conflicting parties receive in this part of the world keeps war alive, killing more victims and sabotaging any future chances of resurrection. The devastation of an absolute defeat always leaves deep physical and psychological wounds on people and land, even if the winning side initiates reconstruction in order to perpetuate its victory. In all peace treaties throughout history, winners have controlled the narratives of the aftermath; they build the monuments, they put up the memorials, they shape the space around their victories. By these means, they not only write history; they shape the future. The important feature in such an act of perpetuation is that it is not just a momentary action, in the category of raising a flag or marking a territory; it takes the form of a plan inspired by a *vision* (be it good or bad). In most cases, this plan seeks to create *character*.

But what is the relationship between overcoming fragility and this ambiguous word 'character', and why do victorious leaders tend to insist on creating it? It seems like a luxury to include such terms in the aftermath of death and destruction. And does it have anything to do with the idea of home, or even answering the 'where to begin' question?

According to the Oxford English Dictionary, the origin of the word *character* goes back to Middle English: from Old French *caractere*, via Latin from Greek *kharaktēr*, 'a stamping tool'. The meaning has evolved from the early sense of 'distinctive mark' to, later, 'a description, especially of a person's qualities', giving rise eventually to 'distinguishing qualities'.[10]

Given that character can refer to distinguishing features or qualities, it is understandable that the term is often carelessly used to describe anything that stands out from its surroundings. I would like to argue that works of the past – the ones we have stopped looking at with a sense of continuity to our present, so we call them 'heritage' – had a character that is often absent from our modern accomplishments. Do the latter lack 'distinctiveness'? Certainly not! Therefore, 'character' must be more than just distinctiveness or distinguishing features.

Khan As'ad Pasha Al-Azm is a caravanserai in Old Damascus which has experienced many ordeals in its lifetime, but this current war wasn't one – at least not directly. With its distinguished design and turbulent history, the building seems like a perfect place to explore the deeper meanings of character. Back in 1757, a powerful earthquake left most of Damascus in ruins and cost the Khan two of its brick domes. Nearly two centuries later, the battles during the French occupation of Syria (1920–46) didn't spare it either – but again it survived, only to fall victim to human incompetence and corruption during an attempt at restoration in the 1980s.

The Khan is arguably the finest and most ambitious piece of architecture in the Old City. It was built in 1752 under the patronage of As'ad Pasha Al-Azm, governor of Damascus under Ottoman rule. The Al-Azm family had climbed the ladder of fame in 1717 to take positions as governors in the name of the Ottoman sultanate all over Greater Syria (Syria and Lebanon). They built incredibly beautiful mansions in Damascus and Hama, but the Khan is an architectural masterpiece. With its 27,000 square feet, it served as a caravanserai for travelling merchants with their loaded caravans and animals; that is why it was built at the heart of the trade centre, Al-Buzuriyah Souk.

Accessed from the souk through a monumental portal decorated with carved honeycomb *muqarnas*, the entrance passage is flanked by two staircases. The building's layout follows the typical Ottoman Khan, with two floors of, in total, eighty vaulted lodging rooms and goods storage rooms surrounding a vast main courtyard space. This is covered with a beautiful arrangement of eight small domes around a larger circular aperture, beneath which is a central marble pool. Today, the aperture has been surmounted with a ninth dome. The moduled domes are supported on four colossal piers that splay, with magnificent continuity, into elegant arches. The walls are made of rubble core embedded in thick lime mortar, dressed with alternating courses of black basalt and white limestone (a technique known as *ablaq*). Although a rigid symmetry is maintained throughout the design, including openings and detailing, the structure never becomes dull or tiring. The architecture of the hive-like space, the play of light and shadow cast by the suspended domes, the continuity with absolutely no interruption – all this moves the eye freely and easily, creating a peaceful experience for the visitor. Even though this is classified as old Islamic architecture, it has aspects that we would normally recognize as contemporary, expressing a timeless organization of space. Masterfully executed, the design manages to leave no void for the eye despite having absolutely no decorated surfaces.

Khan As'ad Pasha Al-Azm in Damascus.

This edifice had changed hands several times and was being used as storage space by a number of shop-owners when, in the mid-1970s, the Syrian Department of Museums and Antiquities decided to intervene. The restoration that began in 1980 included the reconstruction of structural members such as the domes and the four central stone piers of the courtyard, which were replaced with composite ones. A plan was made to convert the building into an arts and crafts centre, giving it a purpose that would take advantage of its location at the heart of the old city; it was expected that little effort would be required to adapt its existing infrastructure to this new role. However, the process of restoration proved to be far from the expected easy ride. According to a 'Technical Review Summary 1986' report submitted by the project reviewer, Professor Okan Ustunkok, to the jury for the Aga Khan Architecture Award: 'The Syrian Ministry of Tourism has stepped in with a prime ministerial decree for taking over the use of the building with a view [to] converting it to a first-class hotel.'[11] This development occurred in the middle of the restoration works, interrupting a process that was far from complete – and then, without any communication with the Department of Museums and Antiquities, the Ministry of Tourism entrusted the completion of the works to the Military Housing Establishment, a front which is involved in executing most public projects in Syria. The whole saga concluded with the Khan eventually being locked up. Shortly before the war, it was proposed as a site for the Natural History Museum of Damascus; but the director of the Khan subsequently stated that work on this project 'has been stopped for unknown reasons...the Khan is being deployed for artistic and cultural events only'.[12] Although the restoration of the building won an Aga Khan award for architecture, it was left with visible electric wiring, carelessly finished plaster patches and other neglected details that currently detract from its aesthetic value. It took the original 18th-century builders only fourteen months to deliver this remarkable edifice, and yet the restoration is still in progress decades after its initiation.

A building like the Khan can be described as both beautiful, in the welcome that it offers, and sublime in its grandeur and scale – an architectural accomplishment as well as a locus for collective pride. No matter how we look at it, the Khan Al-Azm is a real triumph, the kind of building a notable ruling family would choose to immortalize their name with. And it exhibits unmistakable character: not by standing out, but rather by achieving a sense of continuity with nature (in building materials and their effect on different aspects of its design) and with human knowledge (and its interaction with the building materials). On some level, its particular character has more in common with the Land of Hope than with places like the Tower, its slum, or even the 'space capsule' that denied my daughter her memories.

It's a shame that the only way we tend to talk about these buildings today is by grouping them into the flat category of 'heritage'.

Our disconnection from such works seems to stem from the fact that we are no longer able to build in this way. Despite all the new techniques available to us, we are denied that experience of continuity with nature through the use of natural building materials and the means of their production and construction. An awareness that the character of earlier buildings cannot easily be reproduced today fuels the effort to preserve and immortalize these buildings, driving people to cling on to their fleeting traces.

Although the word 'character' has different meanings and is used in a variety of contexts, there is an essential connection underlying them all. In the dramatic sense, when an actor embodies a unique make-up of emotions, movements and reactions in order to portray a complex individual who could have a replica in real life, then the actor has created a character. How do we recognize that this has been achieved? We make a comparison – the character may evoke someone you, the audience, have previously encountered in your own life. He or she may be represented by a new combination of physical and psychological characteristics that you meet for the first time on that stage, but that still make sense in their juxtaposition; such is 'originality'. Whether original or imitated, a fully developed character will provoke our minds, prompting us to make connections and comparisons or draw conclusions – all of which are shaped by our understanding of our surroundings, our emotions and our values. In short, no matter how distinctive the qualities of a performance, unless we are able to relate our impressions of it to our understanding of the world, they will make no sense and will not hang together as a convincing character.

This resonance with one's own worldview is, I believe, what makes the understanding of character independent from the limits of a specific context. When Wright wrote about materials, he explained that 'the character of the wall-surface will be determined by the kind of stone, the kind of mason, the kind of architect. Probably by the kind of building.'[13] He also stated that cement is 'characterless in itself'.[14] Wright's understanding of materials' characters informed his judgment about how to use them. For instance, he praised the Chinese for understanding the character of different stones in a way that allowed them to 'see in them the universe', mastering the art of building with stone as it should be (in Wright's words, 'with real love and understanding') – like the Egyptians, the Maya and the Byzantines.[15] By contrast, he felt that the Greeks had abused it and that Gothic builders, despite their mastery, had treated stone 'as a negative material'[16] with no respect for its character.

Character has order and continuity, and it soothes some of our inner fears by creating and fulfilling expectations. Like an actor's skilful characterization, a building's character *makes sense* in the way materials are understood and used and elements sympathetically assembled – the same way the actor assembles words and gestures and handles props, bringing them together into a coherent whole. All good works of architecture in the past had character. They possessed something we've lost connection with, but still long for. We yearn for that sense of continuity, which seems to have stopped at the wall of the last remaining buildings we describe as 'heritage'.

Inevitably, our judgment of character is linked to our moral judgment and the value system that shapes it. For me, a particularly valuable aspect of the character of buildings of the past is their dignity. If we think of dignity in the sense of maintaining a state of uprightness and resilience, resisting the pressure to collapse beneath the strain of trauma, it seems particularly relevant to older buildings that have survived a war. This quality is related to the way they were built, the materials used, and how all of it has allowed them to survive horrors and damage while remaining standing.

The philosopher Alain de Botton, discussing the related quality of 'elegance' in his book *The Architecture of Happiness*, observes: 'We welcome an appearance of lightness, or even daintiness, in the face of downward pressure – columns which seem to offer us a metaphor of how we, too, should like to stand in relation to our burdens.'[17] De Botton seems to connect elegance to uprightness exhibited in the face of struggle; but we should not forget that dignified, elegant buildings also represent continuity and permanence in the face of imminent demise. They speak to us through this correspondence between moral thought and psychological effect, and consequently they provide us with an anchor by which we settle in – just as the Land of Hope provided an anchor to those last surviving humans. This is one way in which strategies like dehousing, or even the actions of a group like ISIS, strike at the core of our ability to survive: they dehumanize us by depriving us of our dignity. Continuity and diginity are two key values of our heritage. Perhaps that's what made it possible for the fighting powers during the Second World War to agree on preserving the heritage of Christianity by keeping their bombs away from the treasures of Rome. Alas, no such treaties were made to safeguard the heritage of a region like mine.

Since ISIS began barbarically attacking the ancient ruins of the Levant, heritage has become the new buzzword. My first memories of engaging with 'heritage' go back to childhood school trips: watching Western tourists at historic sites, mesmerized by what local children regarded as little more than heaps of tumbled stones. As invisible inverted commas we used to stand between these two contradicting spheres of thought, floating over the heads of two worlds. On one hand, those Westerners, eyes wide, mouths half open, fascinated by the ancient surroundings; on the other, our teachers and various locals, leaning on the columns half-smiling, tongue-in-cheek, taking a picture so as to show the 'foreigners' behind. People used to laugh at the fact that anyone would want to come: 'I wonder what they like here; those funny people!' We grew up convinced that Westerners possessed peculiar tastes. Perhaps it was because they were easily fooled that they chose to visit our country, to wander around these half-standing buildings and dusty objects? Many craftspeople assumed this was so, and charged ridiculous prices for their products that only gullible tourists would be ready to pay. Remembering this now, I can see that we all, locals and foreigners, were reacting to that same disconnection we felt from our past, letting it fall into the 'heritage' box.

One of the main attractions in Damascus is Straight Street, an east–west street that was built by the Romans. It is 1,570 metres long and 26 metres wide, in keeping with typical Roman grid city planning. For many Christians, this place has a special significance; some come from across the globe to visit, or even to buy a house near what they believe will be Christ's alighting place before Armageddon – the Jesus Minaret of the Umayyad Mosque. However, as is the case in almost all 'archaeologically significant' locations in Syria, several layers of sequential civilizations have been built on top of the Roman layer, so that the original Straight Street now sits ten to fifteen metres below the surface.

In 2007, when a decision was made to restore the area, all of the old houses (many of which were archaeologically significant in their own right) were demolished in order to dig up the remaining rows of Roman columns at the sides of the original road. The Islamic fabric of housing and shops that was covering the Roman layer, a blend of different architectural styles from different periods of history, was deemed chaotic and scheduled for demolition. In this way, a genuine example of continuity was condemned to death. The decision was preceded by a heated debate (although not one that involved the public) about which layer to keep, how deep to excavate and – the most insoluble issue – which layer constituted the most significant piece of 'heritage'.

This is just one example of how the same old approach that prevented culture and the publishing industry from wandering off the redlined territory, where discussions of religion, history and complexity are all off the table, was applied to how we look at our heritage and its buildings. And by creating a cultural desert, this process opened the way to radicalization.

The Straight Street in Damascus, 1895.

The Straight Street in Damascus today.

Some local people did understand the value of what we once had, and they had the integrity and devotion to protect and maintain it. But it was not until the destruction began that most of those working on the built environment really started taking an interest in our heritage. Before that point, many Syrians tended to dismiss or despise our heritage, instead coveting what the West had. 'Modern civilization' was the ideal on which we set our gaze; yet we were still weighed down by the heavy baggage of an entrenched inferiority complex and a growing identity crisis. So now, as the West takes an interest – the same West where funds and 'wisdom' reside – heritage has become the alternative. Again we are faced with the crucial question of where to begin.

Today, things have deteriorated far beyond a pre-war situation that was already demoralizing: a time when historic sites, as in the case of the Khan Al-Azm, were left unprotected, vulnerable to looting and attack by vandals; where so-called 'museums' were typically inaccessible, tasteless buildings with a guard dozing off at the front desk; and where the institute of antiquities was just one more place where employees could drink tea and coffee whilst thinking of a new way to run off home before the boss noticed.

We must remember that we didn't just witness the destruction of Palmyra, nor the Umayyad Mosque of Aleppo, not the Crac des Chevaliers in Homs, nor Nimrud's Assyrian city in Iraq; we saw the collapse of complete countries into utter desolation. We did not experience the destruction of the *remnants* of a civilization – we saw the destruction of the social, vocational and moral values that could have equipped us to recognize our 'heritage' for its true worth and build a country as it ought to be.

Today we speak of reconstruction. Some have an eye for investment in infrastructure and large-scale projects, while the more enlightened promote the message of safeguarding heritage. Alas, because we lack the necessary firm ground and stability from which to launch such an enormous mission of reconstruction, we witness even more division. Within the context of civil war, people primarily focus on sectarian division, which is indeed vividly evident all over the cities and towns of the Middle East; however, there is a tendency to overlook deeply rooted conceptual differences of opinion on civic matters, such as the treatment of Straight Street in Damascus. These issues not only represent a real challenge to any serious progress towards a better future, but also hold the key to addressing the very sectarian divisions everyone is focusing on.

All of the work so far on key sites in Syria damaged during the war has followed one principle: 'Every era has its own men.' This arrogant assertion is made by those keen to position themselves as the most distinguished, most influential visionaries of their time. It does not acknowledge that we have lost touch with nature and its building material, or with the accumulation of human labour and its associated knowledge. These are not mere resources that can be manufactured – they are the embodiment of networks of acquired values that mark our own survival.

This guiding principle demands that – as we live in a modern era with new techniques (including 3D printing), new materials, new forms – we could *and should* be implementing them in the so-called 'restoration' process. And it is not merely theoretical; it has been the actual motto of works undertaken in Khaled Ibn Al-Walid Mosque in Homs, in the Umayyad Mosque in Damascus (restored before the war) and in many other places where cement, Italian plaster and similar materials were used in the patching approach. It has also been evident in the intellectual discussions of archaeologists, engineers and heritage experts – not only in practice, but in theory.

In one scenario laid out at a national heritage conference, the question of the future of heritage was discussed through imagining possible solutions to the problem of partially destroyed structures with missing pieces. What if the ancient door of a historic building is missing a handle, for example? What are the choices that must be made in determining how to restore it? In the absence of the specific skill required to make a true replica (or perhaps simply because there is so much at stake; the investment of time and labour required to master heritage crafts could be too much, set against the temptation of quickly attracting global attention), why not simply make a modern one? Or 3D print a copy? Here is where the argument gets its validity: who needs the techniques of the past?! After all, 'every era has its own men'!

Indeed, not only in Syria, but worldwide, it has become a challenge to think of ways to replicate or recreate a valuable object that embodies the principle of continuity. In the absence of any guiding vision, the stage is occupied by voices of division. In Syria we are left with the aftermath of sectarian conflict, which has not only affected us on the level of work ethics and daily encounters, but also influenced how we value works of the past and our ways of investigating history. We are so blinded by ignorance and tribal arrogance that we wish to erase the values of eras we deem to be threatening; we set our own prejudices against their 'ideologies' for no better reason than that 'we were told so'. In my view, this also applies to the Western approach, which celebrates ancient Syrian heritage chiefly because it is considered to be universal and, as such, to belong to all of humanity. Notably, in this context 'ancient' invariably means 'pagan', for it belongs to no religion (as if what divides us is actually religion).

On these grounds we're destined to be forever divided, finding no reconciliation. How, then, will we ever be able to restore or even preserve what remains of our heritage? If we'd taken the time in the past to look closely, we would have recognized that one of the greatest joys for those visiting Syria was that you were able to live alongside our heritage; walk through it, dine within it, maybe buy some of it. We didn't live in a museum, although we could have. For centuries, people in this part of the world understood the worth of what they had inherited or what had existed around them, and built upon it. They used heritage as a living element in the system they constructed around themselves. Whether it was a manufactured object or part of a building, whether it was a construction technique or an ingredient in a dish, they were able to recognize the value of their surroundings and had open minds that allowed them to embrace difference.

Unfortunately, reconstruction in Syria today involves tiptoeing around many fault lines. There is a great deal of focus on fast profit-making, achieving wide global recognition and avoiding losses. It takes time and sacrifice to dig deep and confront such sensitive topics, so instead of addressing the issues, more often than not a prime 'headline-grabbing' location is chosen – for instance, Aleppo – which can then be endorsed as a key focus for the future. Why Aleppo? Simply because it's easiest to work with what and who you already know. Foreign missions have always chosen to focus attention on Damascus and Aleppo, the locations of their embassies and cultural institutions. This, of course, has contributed to the creation of a growth cycle for these two cities, but it does little for anyone living elsewhere.

But haven't we learned anything from this war? Surely we know by now that the sustainability of life in any one place cannot come at the expense of others. The neglected cities and districts that wrought havoc on the rest should provide enough of a wake-up call for us to think twice and take a different route. This time we must be armed with a better cause than simply 'to prove something to ISIS', or even 'to prove something to the West'. Syrians, like any other people involved in rebuilding a country, should not pay too much attention to what the wider world believes we ought to do next. Whatever path the country choses to take with our heritage, it shouldn't be for the sake of anybody or anything other than *our* own appreciation of what we have – our continuation.

But this is no simple quest. To extract life from death, abundance from need, a formula must be found.

2 THE FEAR OF NEED
The Search for Abundance

A sense of security is a cornerstone of our sense of home. Our homes, in addition to being cradles for our memories, our sense of continuity and our accomplishments, must be places where we feel safe – and once we feel secure about our immediate survival, it is the fear of need that takes centre stage.

This is not only the case during war or its aftermath. Even in peacetime, we are constantly seeking reassurance in order to feel safe and secure. We need those feelings in order to become settled and put down roots. Without them, we are adrift in a state of unease.

Just as continuity counteracts impermanence, abundance counteracts need. We find the reassurance we require in places where the land and trees are pregnant with food, water runs fresh and clean in streams and canals, shadows and cool breezes are as welcoming as a wall-bench in the shade, a window frieze, a gentle front step or an open door. Through the way they look, such sights and corners create settings that counteract the fear of need. They exhibit *appearances*, such as beauty, harmony, and the way these interact, and also *realities*, such as variety and abundance.

It may seem uncontroversial to suggest that our sense of security and well-being depends on the absence of surrounding threats, but not everyone sees eye to eye on this matter. For instance, although the Dutch architect Rem Koolhaas acknowledges that we might 'benefit from harmony and beauty' – i.e. the way our surroundings look – he nevertheless believes that they can also give 'a sort of false sense of existential security' and for that reason, according to Koolhaas, 'in every life there needs to be maybe a cocktail of anxiety, disbelief, insecurity, and creativity'. For him the affirmation of security might have a reverse effect. As he puts it: 'I think that to be too certain of your environment and to have an environment that is only affirming a secure situation is probably not a big blessing in the end.'[1]

For some, these comments suggest that Koolhaas feels rather unchallenged by his surroundings and is simply looking for a way to add a little zest to life by way of disruption. Others may judge him for the unsettling effect his modern creations – if they reflect the views expressed above – might have on people who do not have the privilege of a secure living situation in the first place.

For me, Koolhaas's argument recalls the stance attributed to the poet Rainer Maria Rilke by Sigmund Freud. As the two of them were walking in a blossoming meadow one springtime, Freud noticed that Rilke refused to look around him at the beauty of nature; instead, he kept his gaze fixed on the ground, because he was unable to 'forget that all this beauty was fated to extinction, that it would vanish when winter came, like all human beauty and all the beauty men have created or may create'.[2]

The way I see it, both Koolhaas in his comments and Rilke in this anecdote seem to be disengaging from the natural world around them, which is beautiful but inevitably fleeting. Koolhaas displays apathy towards this beauty and harmony, while Rilke cannot bear its dissipation, but in the end their reactions are the same: a looking away.

Many people recognize beauty and its effect on them, but choose to turn away because the weight of its evanescence is too much to bear.[3] If, as I argued in the previous chapter, the condition of enjoyment is continuity, then we can never take real pleasure in a world where everything good is bound to fade away and eventually become extinct. But does that mean we should seek out ugliness and anxiety, as Koolhaas seems to be proposing? Or should we accept the need for the 'suffering of the artist' as a necessary condition of creativity?

I do not believe the answer can be 'yes' to either of these questions. Such an approach makes no more sense than refusing to dine at a hospitable table today, because the same menu might not be available tomorrow. To reject beauty and harmony on the basis that today's 'existential security' might be replaced by a sudden void tomorrow is to give up on the very task of life. It is a self-destructive way of thinking.

On the other hand, there may be a hidden (and perhaps unintentional) warning in the avoidance of beauty; we find traces of a similar line of thought in religious attitudes that link taking the universe's benevolence for granted to the fear of its premature disappearance. Such an understanding has led to the kind of austerity witnessed in Islamic Sufism and Christian Lutheranism. Both regard the world of appearances as a source of distraction from the divine. To enjoy earthly abundance could lead to the spoiling of the disciple's soul; a love of surface beauty might thereby become a barrier between man and his Creator. It seems unlikely that Koolhaas's condemnation of beautiful architecture springs from such a puritanical source – however, it serves to remind us of a motto credited to Mies van der Rohe in the late 1940s, which shaped many modernist buildings: 'Less is more.'

In the period following the Second World War, there was a need to break with a failing system: the ornamented, aristocratic world of class and tradition, having experienced such horrendous losses, had to be replaced by something gleaming and new. More importantly, as in the aftermath of any war, diminished labour forces, capital and housing created the terms on which the future had to be faced. The future had to be *sold*. The trade deal of that century was mass-produced, so its product had to be 'efficient'. Rather like the Sufis and Lutherans, the minimalists of this period preferred their surroundings stripped down to essentials – not because they wished to connect numinously with the divine essence, but because a pared-down aesthetic was 'progressive' and 'rational'.

In some ways, the aftermath of the Second World War was characterized by quantitative abundance – everything was 'booming', from babies to factories to housing units. However, the *quality* of this abundance was far from generous: it was efficient and austere, lacking in substance. Houses became smaller, furniture became stackable and utilitarian. People wanted lighter and 'smarter' objects to adapt to their newly shrunken share of space, but also to claim their membership of the exclusive club of the Modern. The greater the production, the lower the satisfaction. The building and household industries saturated the market first with items that caused problems, and then with other items designed to solve those problems – and the whole competitive dynamic led inevitably to social and material inequality. The old system of class division had been swept away, but in its place was a new system of class division, only this time without the ornaments.

Architects like Robert Venturi responded to the minimalist approach of post-war modernism by reincorporating elements from the classical repertoire, using the familiar in an unfamiliar way. Venturi sought to challenge the monotony – and really, the meanness – of the modernist idiom. When he replied to Mies with the quip 'Less is bore,' his aim was to show that the meagre offerings of minimalists and purists provided no room for the imagination and therefore none for dialogue. But the postmodernism of which Venturi is often regarded as the father (despite his rejection of both the title and the -ism) couldn't offer a solution either, mainly because of its 'false' use of copied elements. One might argue that modernism has, to a certain degree, represented the pastiche of an age in the making. Yet aside from the intellectual debate between the two, modernism has not prevailed over postmodernism on the basis of intellectual superiority; more because it has had the industrial assembly line on its side. Modernism was simply more compatible with mass production than the 'complexities and contradiction' in which Venturi and his followers believed.

Of course, mass production did not begin in the world of building. Cars, rather than houses, led the way – and in due course the buildings made way for the cars. A city that was founded by the French was once the world's centre for that game-changing industry: Detroit. It later became known as Motown, being home to motor manufacturers like Ford and General Motors, but its grand boulevards and rich 19th-century buildings in the European style also earned it the title 'Paris of the Midwest'.

To keep up with demand, Detroit's factories had to attract labour from the countryside. The city expanded, becoming the fourth largest in America by 1920. The infrastructure built for vehicles dictated the nature of the urban fabric – low density and suburban sprawl – while the economic activity segregated workers according to their place in the scheme of production. The isolation of the factory was mirrored by the isolation of the house. As long as the wheels were moving, Detroit had no reason to change its own functional pattern: factories kept increasing production, people kept migrating and forming their own urban cocoons, and the city kept on growing.

For a time, the city was indeed 'booming' – but with the great abundance created at the factory came trouble just as great. In time, Detroit was overwhelmed by riots, leading to the city's inevitable yet unfathomable death. Social historians have explained these events in relation to poverty, inequality, overcrowded housing, layoffs in the motor industry, urban decline, racial segregation and police brutality. But were these truly the causes, or were they in fact symptoms? And if the latter, then what was the real underlying cause?

In my first book, I described how the system of urban factory employment has traditionally drawn upon labour from surrounding areas and the countryside. Newcomers to cities typically inhabited enclaves on their peripheries that became the foundations for a system of segregation. Despite the dissimilar contexts, we have seen in Homs exactly the same chain of events – inequality and division, followed by violence and destruction – that took place so many years ago in Detroit. I want to focus here on the source of the maelstrom that took these two very different cities by surprise: namely, the factory. In both cases, as a source of abundance, the factory lifted the city and its fortunes high, only to drop it hard. I want to explore how such 'Factory Cities' die, why they do so, and whether they can be resurrected.

A city becomes dead when it loses its dynamism, or, in urbanists' terms, its 'livability'. It enters a condition in which businesses dwindle, shops close down, products disappear, prices go up, wages go down – and its inhabitants begin to abandon it, as though jumping from a sinking ship. Such a scenario is believed to have taken place thirteen centuries ago in northern Syria.

On an elevated area of 5,500km^2 between Aleppo and Idlib, referred to as the Limestone Massif, there lies an aggregation of 820 abandoned settlements, mostly dating to the Byzantine era. These are known as the Dead Cities of Syria. Within them can be found more than two thousand churches, in addition to pagan temples, Roman baths, olive oil presses and cemeteries. Like many Syrian remains, they stretch over time from the Aramaic and Hittite to the more recent Islamic.

Despite their name, these UNESCO World Heritage sites are mostly small villages. They exemplify in their rich yet modest architecture a thriving community that depended on agriculture and oil extraction to maintain a hermetic way of life – until, for no evident reason, it withered away. The once prosperous settlements were abandoned for centuries, and have only been partially reinhabited since their heyday between the 1st and 7th century. There is no proven explanation of why they were abandoned but, based on the assumption that olive oil was at the time an international commodity, some speculate that they were occupied by a prosperous and thriving peasant class that slowly lost its influence, perhaps as a result of changes in trade routes. Others have argued that a sequence of earthquakes, diseases and Persian raids devastated the agricultural system and encouraged people to migrate to neighbouring cities.

The mystery is enhanced by two factors: first, the length and nature of the geographical plateau (a hilly limestone strip 140km long and 20–40km wide) on which those settlements were erected, and second, the defenseless nature of the architecture and the apparent lack of city planning or government buildings. The settlements exhibit rural walls and fencing, and stand undefended beside the wealthy and prolific anchorite architecture. Regrettably, the war in Syria has forced displaced people to take shelter in these archaeologically important sites. Some of the buildings are believed to have been ripped apart or dismantled in order to build smaller shelters, while other locations, like the city of Al-Bara, have reportedly been bombed to the ground.

It is more typical in history for a city to be destroyed by something external – an invading enemy, or perhaps a destructive force of nature – than by an internal stroke, like Detroit or the mysterious Dead Cities. What, then, has caused this? The answer lies in what I call Factory Syndrome.

The modern era has been marked by a series of so-called revolutions, each defining an industrial advance so extraordinary as to alter almost every aspect of urban life. First came mechanization through water and steam power; then came the assembly line and electricity; then the computer and automation; and finally, the cyber-sphere and the Internet.

These four revolutions spanned four centuries, beginning in the 18th century. They were driven by ambitions that aligned with my daughter's definition of modernity: 'the least amount of effort for the most amount of gain'. They focused on increasing production by speeding up processes, shortening distances, connecting

Ruins of Serjilla, one of the Dead Cities in Syria.

worlds. For that, they needed inexhaustible sources of energy, and when these dwindled in one place they had to be harvested from other places, even from other countries. Nothing was out of reach: the factory's boilers needed people and energy, whatever the cost. In the context of human settlement, this meant 'bigger distances, and higher densities' – again, just what my daughter described as the basis of social disconnection – and the factory was ready to create the conditions for both of these. Encompassing everything from trains to mobile phones to robots, all four of these revolutions have been in some sense situated in the factory; all have been related to production; and all stemmed from attempts to increase production to the point of saturation.

In 2017, I was invited to speak at the World Economic Forum on the Middle East and North Africa. I remember one of the event's main speakers delivering a speech to a room filled with heads of state and key business leaders. At the end of his speech, the man, whose image was projected in close-up on huge screens at each side of the stage, brightly lit behind his lectern in the midst of the pitch-black auditorium, held his fists high with two arms open and bawled: 'Embrace the fourth revolution! Embrace the fourth revolution!' The room vibrated with waves of enthusiastic applause. I looked around in shock. It felt as if I had been dropped by aliens into a 'take over the world!' meeting on Mars.

I was dismayed by the roar of this new factory, the keys of which were apparently being auctioned to decision-makers and stakeholders. I can only wince at the prospect. Traditionally, as in Detroit, factories have needed large numbers of people to operate; mostly, they have addressed this by recruiting from the countryside and surrounding small towns. But these demographic changes are not natural ones. To work in a factory, you don't really need to become part of the city; you don't need to socialize or get to know people, or even live within the city. All you need is to live near your workplace, or in a place where transport can 'connect' you with that workplace. Your relationship with your colleagues doesn't have to exceed the minimum of social niceties and simple exchanges. You spend your day contained in the box of the factory, performing your daily assignments. To compensate for this isolation, workers in a Factory City tend to stick with their groups: people they know, with whom they may have social attachments that were formed organically elsewhere. This condition arranges life between two poles – *the people I already know* and *the people I don't need to know* –which is an ideal basis for segregation. The city repels the newcomers, and the newcomers unite against it.

The Factory City is segregated not only on the basis of self-selecting groups, but on the basis of class. The wealth that the owners and their circles enjoy is exclusive to them; the class of the rich grows thinner and that of the 'proletariat' thicker. With the growing success of the factory, more labour will be needed, more people will migrate to the city and the population of factory workers will continue to grow. Meanwhile the affluent few become fewer, eliminating each other in the game of competition. The rich, too, tend to segregate: the castle versus the shed, or less figuratively, the centre versus the slum. Of course, there are technological advances and breakthroughs – the factory is followed by the bank and the office building, and more recently by the tech campus – all of which can give rise to their own variations on Factory Syndrome.

A 2017 article in the *New York Times* presented a comparison of the recovery of big US cities from recession with that of smaller ones, in light of the findings of American policy director Mark Muro.[4] Having looked at one hundred of the largest metropolitan areas in the US, Muro concluded that big American cities typically emerge from recession faster than their smaller counterparts. The article discussed how the life of the big city causes the death of the small city, because of the 'accumulation of human talent that is spurring investment and driving innovations'.[5] That is, big cities actually drain small cities of their human resources, just as powerful

The ruined 4th-century basilica of Kharab al-Shams, one of Syria's Dead Cities

countries do to less affluent ones. But the *Times* article makes a distinction between the current economy of innovation and investment (which belongs to the third and fourth industrial revolutions) and the one that existed after the Second World War (which belongs to the first and second revolutions): 'opportunity in the information era has clustered in dense urban enclaves where high-tech businesses can tap into rich pools of skilled and creative people'.[6] Whereas, in the economy of manufacturing, employment growth happened in both large and small cities.

This distinction may give the false impression that there is actually a difference between the Factory and the Campus; or, to put it more clearly, between the industrial revolutions of manufacturing and of information. In my view, there is no such difference. Because we are now producing and consuming at a higher rate than ever before, we have only to ask ourselves 'Where did the Factory go?' in order to realize that we've been on the same track since the first puff of steam. During the manufacturing era, the Factory system was present in cities of all sizes. In both settings it grew larger, with a real impact on the surrounding countryside. At the point of saturation, as happened in Detroit, violence, death and destruction inevitably issued from the suffocating abundance. The city strangled itself.

The age of information has seen things happen on a different scale, but there has been no real change in the pattern. Today it makes more sense to look at the problem globally. Factories did not disappear with the arrival of the internet; on the contrary, they grew so big that we no longer see them! They are now typically based in Asia, Africa, Latin America or the Middle East, where legislation mitigating their impact on climate, pollution and health is relatively loose, tailored to fit the preferences of international investors. In addition, labour and property are typically much cheaper in these areas.

This is all at the core of the colonial history of the factory, which has been driven by the industrial revolutions. The tech campus still functions as a Factory, driven by limitless goals for production, making the product the end and not the means. The process creates a black hole, sucking in the resources of everyone and everything around it until the point of its own implosion.

One might also argue that these descriptions relate to the new liberalism, which presents the market for open competition as part of the natural order of things: as in nature, there are winners and there are losers. Following that analogy, it is supposedly 'natural' that winners keep winning and losers keep losing. But the concept of the Factory refers to more than just the well-known dynamics of the market. It describes changes brought about not only by industrialization and wide-scale production, but by a shift in the emphasis of production. Rather than a means to an end, production became an end in itself.

How did cities function before all of this? And how can our products be a means to an end, and not ends in themselves?

A city becomes a city when it has developed from self-serving production, which is the natural condition of an agricultural economy, into the state of exchange of goods, i.e. commerce. Commerce is the key factor in prosperity and the main component in making a city. No city can thrive in isolation; it needs connections with the surrounding urban centres and the economic flow of the market. However, commerce that is based on *local* consumers' needs is part of what could be called the ecosystem of a city – the cycle that sustains city life, depending on natural systems of supply and demand that are rooted in people's daily lives and activities.

One may ask: but isn't this what all trade is about? Not exactly. Meaningful trade is not about the quality of life *per se*; it's also about the meaning of life. Although it starts by meeting the basic needs of people as individuals, families and communities, it gradually develops a focus on supplementing and enhancing their lives. And these changes in turn act upon and transform our basic needs through a process of conflict and resolution.

In the 7th century, a Chinese admirer of Syria wrote: 'Syria is a place that produces fire-proof cloth, life-restoring incense, bright moon-pearls, and night-lustre gems. Brigands and robbers are unknown, but the people enjoy happiness and peace. None but illustrious laws prevail; none but the virtuous are raised to sovereign power. The land is broad and ample, and its literary productions are perspicuous and clear.'[7] Syria at the time was ruled by the Umayyad. But note how this admirer listed very sophisticated and luxurious items, immediately followed by a description of the prevailing sense of law and order and abundant natural production. Things would not have been this way if Syria's trade had been aimed primarily at outside markets. Instead, the kind of trade depicted here might well serve outside consumers, but it is first and foremost concerned to satisfy the local market. Without such a system, no sense of security or homeland production can be maintained; and, as was the case in Detroit, people will find themselves competing over resources and jobs in order to satisfy the unlimited demands of the international market, always at the expense of the modest local one.

In a local market, the majority of 'consumers' have faces; they are not mere numbers; they are *customers*. Unlike the Factory City, the local market-city thrives with no mass employment. Its people are not employees who could be replaced by robots – they are customers and producers. All traders know that their most precious merchandise is their customers' satisfaction. With this satisfaction comes social manners, smiling faces, understanding and proximity. Although it may be rooted in self-interest, social bonding in such an environment grows organically and evolves into the most essential element in sustaining the life of a city, namely its social fabric. Economic theories of the market start from the premise that a market is composed of self-interested 'rational' choosers, but a local market, among people who interact on personal terms, rapidly softens the 'self-interest' into something even more rational: affection, generosity and mutual concern. The failure to recognize this is one aspect of the inhuman nature of so many economic theories.

Homs, like Detroit, is an example of a city that has lost its social fabric to factories. With the establishment of a petrol refinery, sugar and compost factories in the 1950s, it became an employee city, and with each puff of its industrial chimneys it has been slowly breathing out its life. Mass migration not only brought segregation, but came at the expense of the city's trade. The factory cycle is a parallel cycle to the organic ecosystem of the city, where consumption and production mutually respond to each other. The class division in Homs followed the same pattern described above: the wealthy climbed up and the 'masses' went down, but both groups started abandoning the city, which became a buffer between them.

'Between' (*bain*): Homs has a history with this word. The city is situated geographically on a plain between two mountain ranges, from which it receives its pleasant breezes and nice weather as well as its unique quality of life – something between the settled urban and the nomadic Bedouin. Homs has always depended on its location between the agricultural lands of open, fertile fields and the further arid lands, on which nomadic tribes have traditionally herded cattle. Dairy is the backbone of Homs's famous sweet cookery. However, another key industry in the city also benefited from cattle and land: the textile industry. Thanks to this, Homs managed to recover slowly but surely from one of its lowest points in 1810, with a population of only 10,000, rising to 50,000 by 1911.[8] These were important times in the city's complex history, which we will explore in later chapters; but for now the focus will be confined to its market dynamics, separate from the historical context.

The market (the souk) was the main hub of industry in Homs. The city's growth was marked by the souk's expansion to around 40,000 square metres, ranking the city as a centre of Syria's textile industry. Fine fabrics were manufactured using no fewer than 10,000 looms at a time when the capital, Damascus, had only 2,500.[9] The quantity of these machines compared with the population numbers suggests that almost every family in Homs had at least one loom.[10] This is an example of what the famous American urbanist Jane Jacobs called self-destructive success. In *The Death and Life of Great American Cities*, first published in 1961, Jacobs makes a case for diversity of businesses as an essential element of a city's success. However, she goes on to contend that there is a peak after which this success dips down again; she terms this phenomenon 'the self-destruction of diversity'.[11]

Jacobs insightfully describes a typical form of social behaviour that occurs as people take notice of the economic success brought in by diversity. They observe what is working for others, and they try to copy it. The eventual result is 'excessive duplication', which raises the level of competition and eventually kills the diversity that created the success in the first place: 'The winners in the competition for space will represent only a narrow segment of many uses that together created success. Whichever one or few uses have emerged as the most profitable in the locality will be repeated and repeated, crowding out and overwhelming less profitable forms of use.'[12] This economic triumph is 'hollow', as Jacobs explains, because: 'A most intricate and successful organism of economic mutual support and social mutual support has been destroyed by the process.'[13]

Indeed, the loss of mutual support is the inevitable outcome of industrial competition. Homs's need for labour was the same as Detroit's: an infinite attempt to fuel 'excessive duplication'. The flourishing textile industry in Homs called for hands from the surrounding villages and countryside. So the pattern of the Factory City took shape, and competition over labour destroyed the mutually supportive system to which Jacobs alludes. Homs's textile producers started bidding for labour. Immigration into the city was discouraged by the tight hand of Ottoman policies; in the cities you encountered the centralized power of the Ottoman administration, the tax inspectors and the officers recruiting for military service. Better to stay out of the way, in the distant villages.[14]

The textile industry in Homs was undermined after reaching its economic peak when a group of the most powerful industrialists in the business took the competition to the next level, walking out of the souk and establishing a private company on the outskirts of the city. Using their overwhelming productive power, they effectively played a game of Monopoly with the whole textile market, crushing all competitors. Afterwards, in the 1950s, a still bigger shark – the government – issued an Act of Expropriation and took over the private company, bringing about the end of textile production in Homs once and for all.

To thwart the process of self-destruction, Jacobs proposes three main strategies that she believes can work as a remedy (admittedly with limitations) when combined. The first of these is 'zoning for diversity': conducting a thorough assessment in order to diversify a locality's buildings, height and size to maintain varied usage, and consequently to limit duplication. This in turn needs to be controlled by a taxation system based on profitability. Then she suggests what she calls the 'staunchness of public buildings' – where public and quasi-public bodies should develop a 'penny-foolish but pound-wise' policy in order to defend the urban anchors of diversity in the locality. Finally, she proposes 'competitive diversity', which simply means providing more 'supply' for the required 'lively and diversified city areas'. Although Jacobs recognizes so perceptively what is not working in the city, and why it is not – that is, the human tendency to choose the easiest route to success by copying what is proven to work, until it doesn't – the means she suggests are not really enough, as she herself acknowledges: 'Both of these tools, zoning for diversity and staunchness of public uses, are defensive actions against self-destruction of diversity. They are windbreaks, so to speak, which can stand against the gusts of economic pressures, but can hardly be expected to stand fast against sustained gales.'[15]

Here I venture to disagree with Jacobs. In my view, what she aptly describes as 'windbreaks' could in fact be more effective (and less harmful) than the third tool – more supply for greater demand, which is where the real gales blow from. As Homs and Detroit (and arguably the Dead Cities as well) show us, there is never a balance between supply and demand. There will always be unmet demands and shortages in supply, as long as we look at one of our most essential human needs – the need for home – from the perspective of economic benefits alone. The real threat of the Factory system is that it leaves no place for home. It turns our cities into circles of economic competition, ever growing and ever expanding until they reach a tipping point. Products as well as people are converted into flattened compilations of numbers, whether in banks or in ranks.

How, then, can cities thrive while maintaining healthy trade connections with their surroundings? International trade came into being with the birth of civilization: the ancient system of connection between trading partners was the Silk Road, along which goods travelled and where they rested at certain hubs. The size and destiny of any ancient empire was closely linked to the Silk Road and its life. Because merchandise was not mass-produced, urban centres generally kept things in balance by trading seasonally while remaining more or less faithful to the permanent local customer.

This arrangement was affected by all sorts of considerations: weather conditions, the safety of convoys, the threat of nomad raids. Ancient Persia faced such threats from the north, where the nomads of the steppes were based, from the Black Sea all the way to Central Asia and Mongolia. At the time, these tribes had a reputation for savagery and cannibalism. The Chinese too had recognized the threat that they posed.[16]

Traders had to pay ransoms to ensure the safety of their trade. These payments included rice, wine and textiles, but the most important commodity was the one that gave the trade route its name: silk. For the nomads of the steppes, silk was about status, both socially and politically. So devastating was the effect of nomadic raids that Rome and Persia, who were bitter rivals at the time, made a truce in order to face their common foe. They collaborated in building a protective wall extending from the Caspian Sea to the Black Sea. Despite this, Rome was sacked in AD 410 at the hands of those nomadic tribes, and the Dark Ages began.

The question of the urbanization of nomads was discussed as early as the 14th century by the Islamic historian Ibn Khaldoun, widely regarded as the founder of modern sociology. He discussed 'umran – urbanization – as a process of human settlement. The noun al-'umran comes from the root verb 'amara (to furnish, to give life, to build); it also refers to any act that begets flourishing and settlement.

For Ibn Khaldoun, 'ilm al-'umran (the science of urbanization and settlement) was the true study of human society. Starting from the basics, he considered nomadic life to be the default position of human communities and the origin of every settlement. The perfect minimalism of nomadic existence in comparison to urban people meant they were closer to the good, more courageous and more intensely alive; not 'contaminated with the abundance of urban living'.[17] Abundance brings softness and delicacy, making people too docile, too tolerant and too easily governed – and then, Ibn Khaldoun suggests, they may lose sight of their natural rights.

But the real revelation of Ibn Khaldoun's work is the concept of 'asabiyya: the tendency to live tightly bound to one's own kin and blood. This is the binding force in Bedouin communities, the force behind tribal thinking. For Ibn Khaldoun, it is also the driving force behind kinship – a necessary ingredient in human society, without which there would be no real incentive to aggregate or collaborate. Once detached from the conditions of nomadic society, however, the powerful impetus of 'asabiyya cannot last indefinitely; therefore, those who settle down to form a government in a single place will not establish a regime that endures.

Ibn Khaldoun regards 'asabiyya as both the seed from which nations spring and the seed of their destruction. Division and conflict are inflamed because of it; borders are eroded because of it. The only antidote, he argues, is religion, which turns the blind 'asabiyya from kin to stranger, from the inner kinship group to the outer community. Ibn Khaldoun admits that 'asabiyya is a quality held in disrepute in Islam, but he argues that the object of this disparagement is not the quality itself, but its misuse.

There is no dispute that one of the main accomplishments of Islam in the Arabian peninsula was to put an end to destructive tribal conflicts over the most trivial issues – a verse of poetry, a love affair, a horse race – which had their origins in 'asabiyya. Religion offered an alternative source of self-esteem and human collaborative spirit, rather than kin and lineage: piety, the shared obedience to a vigilant God. However, Ibn Khaldoun was right in his analysis of the dynamic by which nomadic life is governed, and he gave us a rare insight into the nomadic mindset.

He also understood that the transition from nomadic reliance on kinship ties to the contractual bonds that hold a city together was inseparable from the religion that grows between neighbours when they are settled in a single place. Islam and Christianity both recognize that the person you must care for is not necessarily your cousin or a member of your tribe or even of your faith, but your *neighbour* – the stranger you come across, the one who is there in your path, in need of your help or seeking your cooperation.

In the ancient world, cities were often assemblies of people who knew each other. But the city evolved under the impact of trade to become too large for that kind of intimacy, and indeed to become a society of strangers. Yet it was a society at peace – and what made this possible? Ibn Khaldoun is surely right: religion. Not *any* religion, however; rather, the religion which turns all encounters, even those with strangers, into encounters of a personal kind. And this happens easily when you believe that there is a single God watching over you all, that his gentleness and compassion are present in your life and you are being asked at this moment to share them with the stranger whom you face. The very quality that we noted as distinctive in the local as opposed to the Factory economy – market deals that are also personal relations – is promoted by the religion that grows in the city.

Homs, owing to its geographical location, has traditionally had to manage contact with nomadic tribes to its east. On the one hand, the life of the city depended on supplies coming from cattle herding in the vast, arid region that extends all the way to the Iraqi borders, about 450km away. On the other hand, death too came to the city from this treacherous frontier. Whether in the shape of raids or as individual incidents, nomads presented a danger that even the protective wall couldn't completely shut out. The risk of losing valuable possessions, or even a child, was real.

Ibn Khaldoun's concept of 'asabiyya helps us to understand why the city seemed like fair game to nomadic peoples. Tribal 'asabiyya frees the tribe from all rival norms, since outside the tribe there are no rules, no obligations, no shared way of life – nothing other than what an individual might undertake by way of a fleeting commitment. Without buildings, the sense of belonging finds its locus in blood and nothing else.

The fact that nomadic life depends on movement makes it impossible to govern with urban rules. Or, as Ibn Khaldoun puts it, 'movement counteracts the stability by which settlement occurs'[18] – indeed, the condition of accountability is *location*, which is to say *neighbourhood*. Nonetheless, nomadic living is indispensable to the life of cities; herding the cattle away from crops is what nomads do. It is a vital source of livability for both the city-dweller and the nomad. This is an ancient realization that even the greatest civilizations, at risk of being sacked, have tried to accommodate. Islamic religion, too, acknowledged this fact. Instead of trying to impose an abandonment of this type of settlement and consequently endanger the whole urban ecosystem, it identified the root of the problem and encouraged the replacement of 'asabi-yya by a shared piety. In doing so, it regulated nomadic life without interfering in its structure. This is what Ibn Khaldoun partly under-stood; however, he was wrong in assuming that 'asabiyya would simply give way to religion.

The interdependence of the two in Homs was manifested in a smart architectural solution. Rather than being located at the city centre (as would have been more typical), the souk in Homs is located at the far north-eastern end, juxtaposed with its old wall. This loca-tion was influenced by a number of considerations, among them the typology and the ancient site of the massive Temple of the Sun, which in part is currently occupied by the Great Nouri Mosque adja-cent to the souk. According to Nuhad Samaan, a historian from Homs, it was also a strategy by which Homs was able to maintain trade with the surrounding nomadic tribes while guaranteeing its own security. The market's location behind the protective wall with a gate (Bab Al-Souk, the door of the market) connected the city with one of its main sources of living while maintaining its safety, 'pre-venting the Bedouin from entering into the "depths" of the city'.[19] The souk is divided into a network of alleys in the typical Ottoman manner; one of these, the Souk Al-Badou ('market of the Bedouin'), is where exchange with nomads traditionally took place. In this way, movement is directed through the main gate to the main venue of business while the rest of the city is tucked in behind. This urban strategy was colloquially acknowledged in a common phrase: 'in order for (the Bedouin) not to be shown inside'.[20] From a modern perspective, this might seem like an atrocious example of prejudice; but at the time it was devised, it was a solution accepted by both parties, allowing trade and exchange to take place without forcing any change to the essentials of either way of life.

The Factory City looks at every population, every indigenous community, as a possible source of consumers (not customers) and of cogs in the machine. One might argue: isn't human society, at the end of the day, one big machine in any case? It is true that as members of society we are sometimes happy to be that little cog, taking pride at the end of a long working day in having helped to rotate the gears. The problem is that with the advent of globalization and its favourite tool, modernity, the machine has become the dream of the few. Its gears rotate monotonously, generating a consumerist way of life that sells but does not satisfy.

An analogy with natural ecosystems can be made to help illustrate this point. In the US state of Colorado during the early 20th century, the declining presence of the gray wolf in the Greater Yellowstone region was linked to a decline in other flora and fauna. As the predatory wolf population was pushed towards extinction, pressure was taken off the grass-eating elk population, which consequently increased in number and reduced their area of movement in winter. The elk browsed heavily on young willow, aspen and cottonwood plants and this in turn backfired on the beaver population, which needs willow to survive in the winter.[21] To reverse the cycle, researchers with the Yellowstone National Park Wolf Restoration Program aimed to reintroduce the native gray wolf to the park. The plan has worked, helping to restore the number of beavers along with aspen and other vegetation. With the help of the beavers' dams, river levels have also been restored. The pattern of interactions seen here, known as 'trophic cascade', is not unlike the 'urban cascade' of our built environments when essential variations in lifestyle – the nomadic and the rural – are eliminated.

But how can we maintain natural variations of this type if the majority of people are directed into a single mode of living? Although there is currently a sweeping attack on nomadic lands, with the imposition of evacuations and big projects for infrastructure, tourism or industrialization, we cannot deny that many tribes all over the world (even some which are on the verge of extinction) show a pattern of abandoning traditional ways of life for the abundance of the Factory City. Once more, we are faced with the fear of need and the pursuit of abundance. In a pattern similar to the trophic cascade, the pressure of regulations affecting nomadic lifestyles combined with the qualitative abundance of modern housing and employment have had a significant impact. On the periphery of Syrian cities, where social housing projects have been erected, some tribes have found a 'home'; however, in many cases it does not meet their needs. Residents of apartments in these buildings have been known to erect tents of camel hair on the pavements in front of them, preferring to live there while leaving the apartments empty. This tells us something: those people haven't found the home they may have been promised. The city's alluring abundance has turned out to be nothing but a mirage.

Certainly, nomads who live under the open skies, on the other side of nature's soft, concave palm, have to learn how to deal with its coarseness and convexity. This shapes their whole being, as Ibn Khaldoun noted when he described nomadic peoples in the 14th century as raw, tough and pure. They have traditionally been stereotyped as rebellious and intense, but also chivalrous and remark-ably generous. This generosity reflects their unsettled context; being detached and disinterested, they share what they have.

Hatim Altaaey was an Arab poet who lived in the 6th century in northern Hijaz (currently Saudi). He was famous for his inimit-able benevolence. Many anecdotes were told about his incredible acts of generosity, especially towards passing guests – a Bedouin quality of which reports were diffused in poetry. In one celebrated episode he killed his personal mare, a unique Arab breed, in order to feed a woman and her boys who called with an empty dinner bowl in the middle of the night. Hatim showed no reluctance to give away everything he owned for the sake of offering a pleasant and fulfilling experience for his guests, even at the expense of his personal life; reportedly his wife left him after having had enough (or rather, in this case, having none).

Why have the Bedouin tended to go so far in their generosity, despite their often punitive circumstances? Ibn Khaldoun asked the same question: 'Why do those of *'asabiyya* fete others?'[22] He suggested three main reasons: 1) they do it as a testimonial to their glory, or to enhance that glory; 2) they are apprehensive about the reaction of visiting tribespeople, should any dereliction be reported; and 3) they expect similar treatment in return. So was the impressive Bedouin generosity about domination and ambition, political and social status concerns, or self-benevolence? Was it a form of social competition, rather like production in the Factory City?

In fact, unlike the Factory City, Bedouin social competition takes place in the relatively harmless field of direct human relationships – whereas the competition of mass production is impersonal, opening the way to the nihilism that grows around us today. If anything, abundance precipitates society into a state of need – not need for consumer goods, but for that without which consumer goods are worthless: a community of belonging. How can we reconcile this observation with the idea of abundance as the antidote to need? If not abundance, what else will free us from this fear?

Ibn Khaldoun offered us an exemplary outline of the nomadic *'umran* as a social settlement which has no tangible locus, and which therefore needs to compensate by means of the primordial instinct called *'asabiyya*. He recognized the place of religion in social cohesion – but he didn't discuss class or money, for these are products of the city. Jane Jacobs, on the other hand, discusses the city but hardly touches on the issues of socio-psychology that interested Ibn Khaldoun. To understand the dynamics of the urban and the nomadic modes of living, we must combine both perspectives. Although they may grow apart, the ways of the city and those of the nomads are interdependent. The irresponsible upsetting of this interdependence is what has caused the break we observe in the chain of the urban ecosystem: the break from which unfurls the urban cascade. We may now address the question of how the fear of need is exemplified in our built environment, and how a generous city can be achieved. Resolving this will help us not only to restore our homes physically, but to place abundance where it belongs and find the right way of handling it.

What is generosity? It might be described as simply the act of giving; but in fact it is also about taking. Colloquially, where I come from, 'the generous person agrees to take as much as he agrees to give'. This may sound like a contradiction, but its intended meaning is to embrace the idea of sharing. To begin by taking instead of giving is, in a way, to invite trust, and so to accept a relationship. This notion of generosity is really the basis of exchange. Therefore, a generous place – one where our fear of need is dispelled and our sense of home enhanced – is not only a place that gives to us, but a place that allows us to give something back to it.

Despite its flamboyant richness, the embellishment of a 19th-century building in Detroit is as mean, in its way, as any bare block shed in a slum. The former is unable to take, the latter is unable to give – both represent inequality and need. Our cities today increasingly express this kind of meanness. They have turned into places where we are surrounded by tokens of need, both psychological and physical. You can see this in the street benches and shop ledges designed to prevent people lying down, and in the spikes added to the mouldings and frames of buildings so that birds can't perch there. You can feel need in the coldness of the metal chairs in waiting halls, bluntly announcing that you shouldn't outstay your welcome. All of these features are conceived in the name of cleanliness, but their reality is meanness. Because they can be cleaned more easily, people can be paid less, fewer resources can be used and fewer people involved. They are shouting to everybody: *you* stay away! In our modern economy with its modern architecture, everything has a price tag. The city has surrendered its venues to capital, which has turned them into private clubs. Even when those exclusive clubs open their doors, it is in the manner of bait-tossing, luring you into spending.

THE FEAR OF NEED *The Search For Abundance*

Mean, forbidding qualities have invaded the urban as well as the architectural sphere. My brother-in-law lived for more than half his life in Saudi; as a young man, he saw no future in the blocked horizons of Syria on the first day after his graduation. Like many others, he packed his bags and headed for Riyadh, the petrol Factory City in the Gulf. Here – like Van Gogh's coal miners, but wearing suits and tied to desks – countless young men pursued a living without a home. But my brother-in-law carried the nature of Syria in his heart. He befriended a visiting bird that made its way up to the window near his desk. Every morning, he opened the high window of this air-conditioned tower in the burning city heat so as to leave water and breadcrumbs for the little fellow. He admired the bird's free spirit. 'He has wings, free to escape this hell which we can't, but he still perseveres,' he said. 'You see him gasping for air standing on the ledge where I leave the water. He can fly to Syria, where there are trees and water in abundance; to where we cannot fly.' This daily exchange between man and bird was a little oasis of generosity that a window could offer in the soulless desert. But not for long; the architects of the tower decided to enhance its 'efficiency', so they installed a new system of sealed windows that did not open and eliminated the ledge where birds could perch. This change probably affected my brother-in-law more than it did his bird friend.

Twenty years ago, my husband anticipated this experience in thriving Dubai, to which waves of Syrian youths were migrating. Their typical plan was to spend ten years there, accumulating enough money to return and buy a house in Syria's inflated property market. My husband was like the rest of them – featherless, with no family support to offer him leverage – so he was tempted to join the migration. All his friends pressed him to come and see the heaven of Dubai, where 'talents are appreciated'. But he kept resisting. He had his reasons, even if none of these concerned friends understood them. Finally, he agreed to a visit. A friend had arranged an informal meeting in a restaurant with a contact from a Canadian company. 'Would you like to come on board?' the contact asked at one point.

My husband looked at the grass growing in the garden around their table. Reaching out, he moved its roots, exposing a small irrigation pipe. Water flowed from tiny holes all along the pipe in order to water each growing stem; but one hole was blocked, so the grass above it was dead. 'I don't want to live like this grass,' my husband replied. After that, none of his colleagues ever offered him any more job opportunities.

Not all cities are as artificial as those in the Gulf, but the example of these places is spreading worldwide. One only has to look carefully, and the traces can easily be seen. I met a woman in Melbourne who told me that until she graduated from university, she thought there was a charge for entry to art galleries – only to learn later that it had been free all along. I asked what had made her think this way, and her answer was that the galleries 'seemed like that'. How does a building 'seem' to carry an entrance charge? Probably this young woman looked at the richness of the galleries, their fine marble or granite façades, the shiny glass plates or large-scale panels. Maybe she looked at the fountains and statues outside their entrances, at the large empty squares in front of them, and assumed they were like every other building that looks this way – that there must be a price to be paid to enjoy them. Maybe the entrance was too far away from the main thoroughfare, or the passageway was too exposed and she felt intimidated and scrutinized when moving closer to take a look; maybe the façade was too obscure, offering no reassuring glimpse of the visitors or activity within. Maybe there were no trees or birds, so the building could remain as 'clean' and 'pure' as a doctor's surgery. Maybe the building, in its grandeur, seemed unapproachable – *in need*, as if it could not take or give.

In Melbourne, wealth makes no shy gestures. In its central business district, morning queues of Chinese tourists outside a Gucci store are passed by women in high heels and men in smart suits rushing to work, coffee in hand. Tall buildings, gleaming in their high-end finishing, outline the grid network of the city centre. So too do rough sleepers and beggars. In the 1970s, Chinese American architect I. M. Pei collaborated with the Australian practice Bates Smart McCutcheon to create Collins Place, a two-tower complex in Melbourne's central business district, which in 1975 was Australia's largest single building. Its twin 50- and 46-storey towers encircle a vast one-acre, six-storey-high sunken plaza covered in a glazed space frame, the first of its kind in Australia. This complex, which was created after advice from a New York planner, seeks to combine two companies' space in an impressive gesture where luxury and sophistication meet the movement of people.

In the midst of the buzz of the complex's international hotel, offices, shops, cafés, restaurants and cinemas, there is a small room at one corner of the sunken plaza. In less than twenty square metres, with a couple of couches, armchairs, fluffy cushions, two tables, TV, WiFi, chargers and exchangeable books, a free 'living room' has been created. A sign in front of the room says 'Welcome to our free room: free WiFi'. When I visited, I sat there watching the reactions of passers-by; whoever noticed the sign would pause, smile and say 'That's nice!' People using the room were careful not to disturb others, speaking softly and making an effort to be quiet. I noticed that the room had a section for toilets at the back, but it was chained and locked. This suggested that cleaning the space had become an issue; toilets need someone to keep them clean and get paid. It was better to keep this corner somewhat self-sustaining, governed by the authority of the people themselves. It was a friendly, generous spot in the midst of a vast, intimidating commercial space.

Reflecting on this little human corner of the huge, impersonal Collins Place arena, I recalled the architecture of my native country and the way in which it had perpetuated a vision of community down the centuries. And I thought about what we in Syria have lost. Architects in my country who try to revisit the design of Islamic courtyard housing often overlook how generous it is. Their updated versions of the model ignore the fact that the traditional courtyard is not merely a weather-control tool; it is an act of generosity, an extra piece of space with no necessary function, but rather an enhancing role. It is a non-minimalistic, non-nomadic layer, capable of taking as well as giving. Surrounding the courtyard is a traditional array of fruit trees and aromatic plants, providing an array of seasonal flavours and scents. The central water fountain not only cools the summer breezes and moistens the dryness of the winter cold; its depth and surfaces are designed in such a way that the waters play a soothing lullaby in the courtyard space. The porous basalt and limestone blocks absorb noise and extreme temperatures. These details ask for your interaction: the plants that need to be watered, the water that invites you to sit beside it, the stones that entice you to run your fingers across them. They announce their generosity by giving and taking, and for that reason we feel safe around them – we feel at home.

We feel protected when the city offers its abundance not in the form of price-tagged experiences, but in an accumulation of details that are perhaps redundant, but at the same time thoughtful and delightful: a balustrade fixed on a wall next to a steep step, a bench under a willow tree, drinking water flowing from a street fountain, a shaded corner, a fruit tree, an aromatic rose, a running canal, a moulding with birds on it, a decorated window frame or a niche for a potted plant.

The modern, mean-spirited obsession with efficiency and functionality disconnects us from 'home' and exposes our insecurities. So too does the ostentatious display of wealth on buildings, which makes meaningful exchange with our surroundings impossible and prevents us from feeling at home. The difficulty is in part financial: who will pay for a generous city? And those who pay, who will pay them back?

The Islamic city's answer to this problem took the form of the *waqf* (plural *awqaf*), or endowment. The literal translation of this

Collins Place, Melbourne.

term is imprisonment, or prohibition; in other words, a *waqf* means that a property is given to a certain charitable or publicly necessary cause, and any other use of it is prohibited. From this rule there developed a wide spectrum of legislation in the Islamic era. It played a part in a flourishing economy and the creation of generous cities, through the founding of schools, colleges, hospitals and religious establishments.

Although the *waqf* in its original form shared some legal similarities with the charitable trust, as a voluntary financial system for property management it had a different, eternal character, being strictly tied to the original intention of the donor. It sprang from religious beliefs that stressed the importance of charity and giving, seeking no earthly reward. In no sense was it (as many trusts that once created the great cities of Europe have become under English law) a kind of tax dodge whose main purpose was commercial. Once a property was endowed under Islamic law, it could not be sold, and the purpose for which the original owner established it could not change, even after his death. The profits that came out of a *waqf* had to be spent on the specified beneficiaries, which included people in need, travellers and passers-by, orphans and so on. For example, a person might create a *waqf* of his orchard so that all its products became an endowment to people in need; or it could be a library, a house or a school. All of these are examples of *awqaf* that expanded and flourished independently under the management of an independent, non-profit and non-governmental body, which had a special immunity to corruption owing to its religious detachment from personal benefit.

This system made possible the physical generosity of Islamic cities in their heyday and the preservation of various historic layers of their buildings. There were *awqaf* for broken chinaware that you could replace with new ones, for removing stains from clothing, for the support of ageing animals that were no longer wanted by their owners, and so on. Institutions like this create a vital distinction between civil society and the state. They enable ordinary people to govern their affairs independently and in a public-spirited manner, without fear of intrusion from government. Hence they were essential to the freedom and generosity of the Islamic city. In this way, the *waqf* was an intrinsically city-making force.

To understand how much of this has been lost, consider the *waqf* of the Green Meadow in Damascus, which was once dedicated to sick and ageing animals. Later, the land was confiscated and transformed into a site for the Damascus international fair: a location for conducting international business! Later still, a project called Massar ('Trajectory') was created as a learning centre for children, designed by the Danish firm Henning and Larsen. Its design was supposed to be inspired by the atmosphere of the old alleyways, with a symbolic embodiment of the Damascene rose shape. In order to fulfill this vision, the expropriated *waqf* land was left empty around the centre so that it could be landscaped; but in an area of 16 hectares (almost the size of 25 football pitches) as a 'public space', you would have needed a good pair of binoculars and a scooter just to find someone to talk to. In any case, as a result of bureaucratic delays followed by war, the building was never completed. Its bare rose structure now stands in a deserted meadow of dust.

After the fall of the Ottomans, the French and British occupied the territories lost by the crumbling empire. One of the most sinister amendments they made to existing laws was to alter the whole nature of the *waqf*. British colonial authorities incorporated a commercial dimension into the system and 'modernized' its management structure; they were determined to end the *waqf* once and for all because they recognized the undefeatable, empowering impact it had on society. First, the independence of its management had to end; so that responsibility was handed over to a government body. Then the trans-oceanic connections of the *awqaf* in various Islamic countries had to be disconnected. Finally, decrees and new laws ensuring official control over *waqf* endowments had to be enforced.

The French, in their colonies, followed the same strategy. In Syria, as in Algeria and other occupied territories, they cancelled the family *waqf*; they also removed the independence of the *awqaf* and assigned a government body to manage them. Their laws allowed government to expropriate *waqf* properties and change their character and purpose. And these policies have been continued by their Ba'athist successors. In Syria today, the Ministry of *Awqaf* is one of the most corrupted and failing ministries. Many of the decaying buildings and vacant, derelict properties puncturing the cities belong to the *awqaf*. The religious buildings they own now – namely mosques and their schools – have lost their charitable purpose and been turned towards the corrupt policies of gov-

Massar Learning Centre in Damascus. The project's construction works are suspended in this current state.

ernment officials. This is one of the main reasons why civil society in this part of the world is so crippled, and why the road of city planning and heritage preservation is so full of bumps. Unlike government social programmes and stumbling financial schemes, the *waqf* is not only a tried remedy for housing and public and civic maintenance, it is an antidote to the culture of debt and the consequent seizure of power by the banking sector.

A flicker of hope was Homs's charity Al-Bir, an independent body that was credited with eradicating homelessness in Homs before the war. This charity was founded in 1956 with a vision of creating a 'society clear of poverty, ignorance, and illness' in response to the social repercussions of the French occupation, which ended in 1946.[23] *Bir* in Arabic refers to all good and pure deeds. No government programmes were used, and no fundraising or additional taxes were enforced; the charity depended solely on anonymous donations. Through the system of *waqf*, it established and built many foundations including a rehabilitation centre for the blind (1959), a nursing home (1960), a craft institute for girls from poor families (1962) and an office to combat begging (1970). Thanks to the work of Al-Bir and to the system of *waqf*, Homs became the only city in Syria with 0% homelessness. Those who had no home were given homes, those who needed a job were found a job, those who were ill were treated and those who were using begging as a 'profession' were prosecuted.

But when the war hit in Homs, the atmosphere of increasing distrust and censorship had a significant impact on the charity. Much of its volunteer work had to stop because of the forced migration of young people and the intense suspicion with which the state regarded any movement of funds. In addition, the growing presence of international organizations and NGOs undertaking humanitarian work meant that the local system and its informal, improvised way of functioning lost some of its appeal for the younger generation. I remember hearing one young architect who was volunteering with the charity express his frustration with its 'elders' – men in their sixties and seventies who often had to be coaxed into action by their younger colleagues. The young man was frustrated because his older colleague didn't open his emails! I said: 'So don't send him an email – you work in the next room, go and talk to him.' But the young man seemed equally unimpressed by my old-fashioned suggestion.

The Al-Bir also had to defend its reputation in a context of increasing corruption among more recently established organizations and NGOs. Despite its best efforts, it ultimately became just one more organization that people had to decide whether to trust.

It is perhaps worth returning here to the story of Detroit, which saw the positive effects of charitable work in the form of its 'Grand Bargain' of 2014. This succeeded in keeping the city's collection of art in the Museum of Detroit, a charitable organization managed by the Founders' Society; it also rescued Detroit from bankruptcy and saved many workers' pension schemes. Since then, the city has been making every effort to revive itself, attracting well-known architects to work on big projects and launching a number of important rehabilation schemes.

Yet Detroit hasn't quite escaped from the danger zone. It is positioned on the interstate corridor from Indiana to Alabama, a location where Factory Syndrome is intensely felt; according to statistics compiled in 2017, there are 'more than 15,000 industrial robots in place or 8.5 per 1,000 workers...more than three times the number of installed robots of other metros'.[24] The cycle that was created by the automobile industry has not yet been broken. As Mark Muro observes, 'automation will resemble other economic changes in that it will touch down in disparate communities in disparate ways'.[25]

How can we mitigate the effects of such changes? We need a generous city, one that brings people together as neighbours without 'asabiyya – one that lays the foundations for exchange, in every sense, and has little room for the fear of need. The waqf system is one example of a perfect tool with which to accomplish such generosity and challenge the greed of the Factory.

Of course, I'm not imagining simply pulling the plug on industry, if such thing is even imaginable. What I am saying – and what I hope this chapter has shown – is that the Factory City is a failing system, demanding endless resources that cannot be acquired in sustainable ways. Injustice and inequality are inevitable in such a set-up. Modernity can and should stop serving the Factory as it did in the aftermath of wars. Modernity must learn to be generous, to belong to the Land of Hope instead of the Tower; for our accomplishments tie knots with our possessions in order to make us who we are. If they are created with a sense of continuity and generosity, our buildings can grant us dignity and security, and these attachments will help to tie us to the place we call home.

3 THE FEAR OF TREACHERY
Finding the Exit

Flocks of birds, shoals of fish and herds of wild cattle all follow patterns in their movement: they seek food, a hospitable climate and an abundance of resources. But this search is not without risk. The threat of harm from treacherous weather and predators compels all of these creatures to behave according to the herd instinct.

The quality I will refer to here as *treachery* – the closest English equivalent, I believe, to the Arabic *ghadr* – is associated with certain spatial characteristics, and with darkness and concealment. It combines threat and the betrayal of trust; it breaks out from still and silent cover with no prior warning. Humans carry a primitive fear of it, just as animals do. In our own search for abundance we are like those herds, challenged by the threat of treachery. Before we can settle somewhere, we first need to identify threats and eliminate their sources. This requires us to understand both the psychology of treachery and the qualities of the space where it resides. These two intertwined factors are closely related to our quest for home.

In general we trust what we see, so treachery must come from a blind spot. Darkness, deepness and vastness are all examples of the limitless, which betray the limitations of our trusted sense of sight. We fear what we do not know, mainly because we fear the treachery of what we cannot see – whether in reality or in imagination.

What we actually see is a construct of neural networks and unconscious images. Whatever is received by the physical eye passes an impression to the mind's eye, and this impression is malleable in the light of memory. In his book *The Poetics of Space* (1958), the French philosopher Gaston Bachelard linked feelings of settlement and dwelling with the inner image of one's childhood house: 'The house we were born in has engraved within us the hierarchy of the various functions of inhabiting.'[1] In this 'oneiric house', as Bachelard termed it, 'dream is more powerful than thought'.[2] This power of dream over thought is actually the power of remembered feelings of love and fear, which we experience as children in that 'oneiric house', over the real-time image of the present:

> ...and so, beyond all the positive values of protection, the house we were born in becomes imbued with dream values which remain after the house is gone. Centres of boredom, centres of solitude, centres of daydream group together to constitute the oneiric house which is more lasting than the scattered memories of our birthplace.[3]

Bachelard breaks down the oneiric house, the place where a person first meets the world, into two principal 'connecting themes'. The house is imagined as 1) a *vertical* being, and 2) a concentrated being, appealing to our consciousness of *centrality*.[4] Unlike the horizontal modern 'flat', Bachelard's house is a vertical and centred unit that stretches between two poles – the sky and the earth – and embraces and protects the child from the hazards of the outer world. Moreover, his house is a typical vernacular house. It links to the sky with a pitched roof to shelter from the weather, under which the attic resides; and it drills into the ground with a basement as a fortified foundation.

For Bachelard, as children, we experience both safety and danger within this 'dual vertical polarity'[5] – between the attic, a symbol of protection and shelter from the weather's forces which affords the 'rationality of the roof', and the cellar, the *'dark entity'* which 'partakes of subterranean forces' and where we connect with the 'irrationality of the depths'.[6]

In the attic, fears are easily 'rationalized'. Whereas in the cellar...
'rationalization' is less rapid and less clear; also it is never definitive.
In the attic, the days' experiences can always efface the fears of night.
In the cellar, darkness prevails both day and night, and even when we
are carrying a lighted candle, we see shadows dancing on the dark
walls....In our civilization, which has the same light everywhere, and
puts electricity in its cellars, we no longer go to the cellar carrying a
candle. But the unconscious cannot be civilized.[7]

Closer examination of Bachelard's house reveals that what our inner child fears is nothing other than treachery. He fears the darkness of the cellar, even holding that imagined candle which might be blown out at any moment, leaving him trapped underground, where behind the walls is 'the entire earth'.[8] For the mind's eye, this means facing the treachery of the unknown – getting stuck with no exit behind buried walls. Yet Bachelard insists on the importance of the cellar for stability, for the dreamer's house 'wants the undergrounds of legendary fortified castles'.[9] Once again, the unconscious is faced with the fear of treachery: the treachery that can compromise our safety, be it a thunderstorm or a concealed villain. Why else does one need a 'fortified castle'? In comparison, the attic is less treacherous, for it offers the possibility of exit. Faced with the threat of attack, a person can jump from the window or climb onto the roof.

In my view, the importance of Bachelard's 'dual vertical polarity' stems from the balance it offers to the psyche: confining yet fortifying stability on the one hand, and liberating yet sheltering verticality on the other. The centrality it offers to the 'dreamer' is one of equilibrium, marking the place of the human being among the forces of nature and the surrounding world.

What does this mean for the designs of our residences today? Does it mean, for example, that we cannot inhabit the modern flat in the way that we inwardly inhabit that 'oneiric house'? Before we address this point, let us first look at what architecture does.

If we strip architecture to its core, we find that what it does is *define boundaries*. Whether playing with space or with details, architecture uses boundaries as its fundamental organizing grammar. The window, the door, the column and so on are forms that take shape by tracing boundaries. So is the ceiling a dividing plane between upstairs and downstairs, and the wall a plane between outside and inside. The very concepts of 'up and down' and 'outside and inside' are defined by boundaries – by where and what we cross as we move from one to the other.

In that sense, architecture is essentially the art of defining the boundaries within which we humans are placed and across which we move. Our interaction in, between, and through these boundaries is influenced by their shape, their thickness and their permeability. Bachelard's oneiric house derives its vertical centrality from enclosing the living space and its inhabitants between two thresholds: two boundaries that centralize the inhabitants and channel their relationship with their surroundings. Indeed, the attic and the cellar were able to create what Bachelard termed a 'dual polarity' because they acted as boundaries between the living space (the house), and its surroundings (the universe). Primitively, we are placed between two major entities: the sky above and the earth beneath. Whatever we build, we build it over the earth and under the sky. We cannot escape these boundaries. So we add to them what defines our relationship with them, avoiding their hazards and accepting their gifts.

The design of the traditional Islamic house also adopts this 'dual polarity' in its vertical orientation, with the living quarters on the ground floor and the private rooms upstairs. However, at its heart lies the courtyard, creating an open and direct relationship with the sky. Following the fall of the Ottoman Empire, the advent of the colonial powers, globalization and finally the wars of the so-called Arab Spring, this model of the house gave way to the modern apartment – the 'flat', a term that accurately reflects what has happened to us. We have suffered a radical break from the architectural idiom that arose in response to our way of life and perpetuated it in the boundaries that we understand. In the West, on the other hand, the modern flat's use was amplified by the building industry in the wake of the two world wars. The high demand for housing during this period was not only the result of destruction; it also reflected an increase in rural migration towards urban centres in response to industrialization, echoing the pattern of the first two industrial revolutions. A new world was born: new ideals, a new society and a new kind of money-making. This hungry industry ate up cities around the world, in both the 'developed', which is to say colonizing, and the 'under-developed' or colonized worlds.

Nonetheless, there was a major difference between these two worlds when it came to transformations of the countryside. In places like Syria, the vernacular rural house – originally shaped by two variables: the local building material and the micro-climate – was replaced almost completely by block building, a kind of construction entirely divorced from the surrounding natural world and a by-product of transformations taking place in the city. In the European countryside, vernacular models were still appreciated and made room for; not so in Syria.

Not long ago, I was involved in a joint event in Melbourne with an Australian artist who was assembling drawings made by Syrian refugee children into a book. The children had fled or migrated from different parts of Syria. They were asked by the artist to respond to some questions by drawing – mainly 'What does home look like?' The captions underneath their drawings indicating their homes of origin revealed that the mix covered rural and urban areas, as is the nature of migration caused by war. I was struck by the fact that none of these children drew their 'real' homes. All of them drew gabled detached houses – houses that looked like Bachelard's dream house, and nothing like the houses in which those children might have been brought up.

There are a number of possible explanations for this. One is the basic icon made familiar by cartoons and illustrations, in which a square topped by a triangle expresses 'house'. Moreover, Syrian society in general teaches 'ideal forms' rather than free expression: whether at school or at home, children must perform as expected. They must colour rigidly inside the outline, copy exactly the same shape, write perfectly on the line, precisely memorize a text, and so on. From the cradle, the imagination of the Syrian child is suffocated by ignorant social competition and parental selfishness. This could appropriately explain the primitive quality of the collected drawings in the book. Indeed, the children shyly used little or no colour, had no structure for their pictures, scattered disjointed elements to fill up the page as if putting words in a sentence to say: This. Is. The. Answer. To. Your. Question.

However, I believe there is more to it than that. I think that the children were unable to draw their homes because they didn't have homes. The experience of living in a flat had failed to establish itself in their imaginations. It had failed to impress its form onto their consciousness so as to give them what Bachelard described when he wrote that 'a house is constituted of a body of images that give mankind proofs or illusions of stability'.[10] The flat offered no *stability* and therefore generated no body of images that could find their way onto that blank sheet of paper.

In principle, a flat is a horizontal slice of space that orients the inhabitant towards the surroundings that are parallel to its plane: it offers four horizontal directions, but no vertical axis. The connection with the earth and sky is lost. Something else is lost too, which is the boundary of ownership. If one of our refugee children wanted to draw their apartment, they had to draw the whole block and then somehow indicate which end of which floor was theirs.

Of course, the higher the flat, the blurrier the boundary gets, both for the physical eye and the mind's eye. And the further one goes from the ground, the more difficult it becomes to exit. In that sense a skyscraper is the most treacherous of all buildings, since the exit disappears from both ground and sky. Its roof is disconnected from those of its neighbours, so there is no way to flee from fire, and the ground is far away and unreachable in an emergency: witness the tragedy of London's Grenfell Tower, ravaged by fire in 2017 with the loss of many lives. In *The Architecture of Happiness*, Alain de Botton paints a vivid image of buildings around which we feel safe: 'We appreciate buildings which form continuous lines around us and make us feel as safe in the open air as we do in a room. There is something enervating about a landscape neither predominantly free of buildings nor tightly compacted.'[11] De Botton's buildings – which in their 'continuous lines' create an embracing circumference, not too tight and not too loose – make us feel safe for one reason: they speak to our fear of treachery. They are mapped between the earth and the sky, vertically in relation to the horizon, and horizontally in relation to each other and to us. They succeed in making us feel safe only when they cover our backs.

De Botton touches upon this human vulnerability when describing a jammed street: 'Le Corbusier...forgot that without pedestrians to slow them down, cars are apt to go too fast and kill their drivers, and that without the eyes of cars on them, pedestrians can feel vulnerable and isolated. We admire New York precisely because the traffic and crowds have been coerced into a difficult but fruitful alliance.'[12] This alliance is only fruitful because it fulfils the requirements of psychological safety, namely to have the 'eyes of cars' watching over the backs of otherwise 'vulnerable and isolated' pedestrians. It is the same coverage to our backs that we seek even from chairs: 'It isn't sufficient that our chairs comfortably support us; they should in addition afford us a sense that our backs are covered, as though we were at some level still warding off ancestral fears of attacks by a predator.'[13]

We carry this primitive fear of treachery everywhere we go – whether standing in a public square or sitting in a study with our back to the door. We ward off those ancestral images of an attacking predator, along with the more recent ones of a prowling burglar, whether in a lonely, dark alleyway or on the empty pavement of a wide highway.

Architecture depends on creating boundaries that do not intimidate or separate. This is an artistic challenge that revolves around a paradox: to use what in essence is an outlining tool, but without isolating or prohibiting access to either side. Too many architects take refuge in the 'sheer edge': the clear-cut boundary, which was introduced through the industrialization of building and became a distinguishing feature of modern architecture in comparison with older styles. Mass-produced materials and geometrical ground plans have come to dominate architectural practice; as a result, modern buildings often refuse to join to their neighbours, stand opposed to them, cut cleanly away and show no apparent desire to weave themselves into the city. Edges in older styles of building were never sheer – they were softened with mouldings and crowned with details that cast their shadows across the surface.

The distinction between the 'sheer edge' and the 'soft edge' points to the ways in which architecture can capture or violate our human sense of belonging. We seek resemblances between ourselves and our buildings in order to feel safe around them: a reassurance against our fear of treachery. But it is not the physical resemblance that gives us reassurance, rather the *behavioural* one. A building with a soft edge protects our backs: it is not 'refusing to join'. Psychologically we lean against it, nestle into it, jostle beside it as we do in a friendly crowd.

The Islamic house that has Bachelard's dual polarity on the inside has a soft edge too on the outside. The façades of such houses, joined in continuation with minimal interruptions and only slightly differentiated in appearance, hold no gestures back in offering protection to all passers-by. Those gestures can be read in the soft edges, whether in the texture of the natural stone (cut with character), the cool shadows of window bays or the bowed front doors one step down the alleyway. Those edges invite our senses to be involved. The stone feels warm in the cold and cool in the heat. The courtyard houses are so aligned as to break the wind into breezes and tunnel the heat into cool currents. The wall that looks as if it is bending in order to carry the jasmine across it, and the courtyard from which the lemon and the fig stretch their heads towards the street, offer the best 'welcome' that any doorstep could make. There is no place for this kind of edge in the factory-made curtain walls, the pressed glass sheets, the sheer metal-framed doors that carve the space of our streets, like butcher's knives held to our backs.

The role of the architect – at least, one who is concerned with building homes for people where they can feel safe and protected – is to understand these fears and overcome their negative effects. The significance of how architecture is perceived is explored in the work of Kevin Lynch, who was an American urban planner and associate professor of planning at MIT. Lynch wrote about the qualities of urban boundaries as an important aspect of how we perceive the city – as expressed in the title of his 1960 book, *The Image of the City*.

For Lynch this 'image' was made up of five elements – paths, nodes, edges, districts and landmarks – that combine to form the 'mental maps' we use to understand and navigate our urban environments. His description of each element is valuable but the discussion of edges ('boundaries between two kinds of areas')[14] is arguably his most important observation when it comes to the question of how the city *works*.

Lynch distinguishes between 'strong' edges – impenetrable, visually prominent, displaying continuity of form – and 'weak' edges, which lack such qualities.[15] A strong edge can be a prohibiting boundary, dominating the space it defines, often making it difficult or even impossible to penetrate. Such edges can be off-putting, leading people to avoid them so that an abandoned and unsafe area develops; this is what Jane Jacobs, in her discussion of

Lynch's work, calls a 'vacuum'. However, not all strong edges are impenetrable. Some are not 'isolating barriers' but 'uniting seams' that, in the right circumstances, can succeed in pulling residents together.[16] How does this pull happen – what attracts people towards a boundary? And why are boundaries more prone to creating vacuums than other urban places?

Water edges, woods and large parks, railways, highways and even campuses are examples of urban boundaries whose firm and continuous edges can easily drive their surroundings into decay. Lynch focuses on their visual and aesthetic aspects while Jacobs tackles them from the analytical perspective of the urban economy, but they agree on more or less the same strategies by which a 'barrier' can be turned into a 'seam'. In discussing this, both writers use the example of the waterfront. Lynch summarizes his point of view in terms of two main aspects, *visibility* and *accessibility*:

> An edge may be more than simply a dominant barrier if some visual or motion penetration is allowed through it – if it is, as it were, structured to some depth with regions on either side. It then becomes a seam rather than a barrier, a line of exchange along which two areas are sewn together. If an important edge is provided with many visual and circulation connections to the rest of the city structure, then it becomes a feature to which everything else is easily aligned. One way of increasing the visibility of an edge is by increasing its accessibility or use, as when opening a waterfront to traffic or recreation. Another might be to construct high overhead edges, visible for long distances.[17]

Jacobs, too, believes the solution lies in revealing the use of the boundary, making it visible and approachable: 'Penetrations into a working waterfront need to be right where the work (loading, unloading, docking) goes on to either side rather than segregated where there is nothing much to see.'[18] But she recognizes that some boundaries are too resilient for this approach to work; for instance, in the case of large-scale expressways, campuses or parks, the size of the barriers can be too enormous to suggest they have another side.

> The only way, I think, to combat vacuums in these cases is to rely on extraordinarily strong counterforces close by. This means that population concentration ought to be made deliberately high (and diverse) near borders, that blocks close to borders should be especially short and potential street use extremely fluid, and that mixture of primary uses should be abundant; so should mixtures in age of buildings. This may not bring much intensity of use right up to the very borders themselves, but it can help confine the vacuum to a small zone.[19]

In short, both Lynch and Jacobs propose that edges should convey a message to the passer-by: 'There is nothing to be afraid of: your back is covered!' This reassurance creates purposefulness and offers meaning to potential visitors. Edges represent the end of one place and the beginning of another – the zones where directed movement fades away – so there must be persuasive reasons for people to approach them.

It is not surprising that both Lynch and Jacobs refer to waterfronts in their discussion of edges. Almost all thriving ancient cities were built next to water, which was essential to transport, agriculture and trade. These in turn were essential to the cities' growth: agriculture is inhaled in the village and exhaled as trade in the city. Only later did technological advances in transportation turn waterfronts into water edges, in need of the interventions described by Lynch and Jacobs.

Of course, both Lynch and Jacobs were writing primarily about the rapidly developed American city, not the organically grown European or Middle Eastern city. The element of time is key here because it allows for human activity to take root. Market streets gradually grow into quarters; public buildings place walls and doors along the street; religious buildings make sacred spaces in front of them. In this way they become more permeable than the rigid boundaries Jacobs and Lynch refer to. One of the perils of the Factory City pattern is the constriction of this element of time, so that permeable boundaries (seams) have no chance to develop and rigid edges (barriers) dominate the urban landscape.

The English philosopher Roger Scruton notes our reliance on boundaries of various types – from clothing, manners and social courtesies to rights and legal systems – to help us navigate the world. Some of these boundaries, he reflects, are permeable while others are more solid, and '[t]hese distinctions have their counterpart in the language of architecture':

> Walls can be forbidding, inviting, permeable or semi-permeable. Doorways may be ceremonious or perfunctory. Exteriors can be accommodating or severe. And the language here is integral to the way in which a building fits to its neighbours. In this way the art of the boundary, through which we learn to accommodate our desires and places to those of our neighbours, is replicated in the sphere of architecture, and illustrates the way in which aesthetic education and moral education are rooted in the same human need – the need to live in harmony with others, and to reconcile individual ambition with a shared sense of home.[20]

How do we navigate the boundaries of our built world? My travels following the publication of *The Battle for Home* gave me the opportunity to discuss its themes with international audiences. One common misconception I encountered was that in criticizing urban segregation, I was advocating either a completely open city with no process of social filtration – what you might call a 'big party' kind of place – or alternatively, a place where people labelled as part of different groups would each be encouraged to occupy a slice, with shares equally divided between them – what I think of as a 'big salad bowl'. People also spoke of a 'melting pot', a heterogeneous place that has 'melted' into apparent homogeneity. But does the melting pot really exist? Do boundaries actually dissolve?

In my view, both the 'big party' and the 'salad bowl' eventually end up becoming modes of segregation, as the groups involved seek self-agglomeration. On the other hand, the 'melting pot' is as likely to produce a confused mass of isolated individuals as a genuine community. The fact is that the human mind depends on filtration in order to make sense of its environment – where 'make sense of' boils down to 'feel safe in'. Humans generally fear what they do not know, and in particular we fear the treachery of the 'other'. Hence people typically gravitate towards who and what they know, and in order to achieve this they resort to social filtration.

In order to understand social cohesion, therefore, we first must acknowledge the need for boundaries and recognize that it stems from our fear of treachery. Different groups of people are able to merge boundaries and gain trust by means of daily interactions which are, in many cases, based on social boundaries – the manners and courtesies noted by Scruton. In this way, boundaries that were initially erected for safety become permeable and therefore instruments of trust.

In an article for the digital magazine *Aeon*, social anthropologist Farhan Samanani discusses the issue of sharing public space, particularly in the context of a heterogeneous urban community. London is a perfect example of a sprawling city to which people migrate from all over the world. Like all *megalopoleis*, it exhibits every kind of segregation: class, religion, origin and so on, with a 'melting pot' at the centre. Samanani's article focuses on the specific neighbourhood of Kilburn, which he calls 'either one of the most vibrant or one of the most dysfunctional neighbourhoods in London':

> Clustered in the north-western part of the city, the area has been a swirling mix of cultures for more than 100 years, starting with Irish and Jewish migrants in the late 19th and early 20th century, up to more recent arrivals from the Caribbean, Latin America, Sub-Saharan

Africa and eastern Europe....When Kilburn's residents do come together in public, clashes often ensue.'[21]

This is a quintessential feature of modern cities, in which mixture does not necessarily mean harmony. Instead of the sought-after melting pot, the reality is often no more than a salad bowl. In response, we hear cries for a more inclusive design for cities – but what does 'inclusive' really mean? The word is mostly misunderstood in 'salad bowl' terms, with every group granted its 'right to the space'. This is the main point highlighted in Samanani's piece, which shows how public space is fragmented as different groups lay claim to it at different times. Between open holiday barbecues, dog walks in the park, young hipsters, loud music, mothers with an arsenal of baby prams and so on, Kilburn's park and street become more a confused jumble of private rights than a shared public space.

The question Samanani raises is, who owns the right to the space? How can users of different ages, needs and convictions mould their rights to use the public space into one common ground, without ending up in conflict? From his perspective, architecture alone is incapable of addressing this problem: 'It's not our architecture that needs a refresh, but our habits.'[22] And he's partly right in this. It is true that what we broadly refer to as 'inclusive architecture' is incapable of seamlessly bridging the colossally distinct worlds brought together by migration. We do not become inclusive merely by collapsing boundaries. It is not architecture that is at fault, but rather our own off-target understanding of 'inclusivity'.

Samanani's conclusion is accurate and simple: we need to acknowledge our mutual dependency in order to find a way to live and work in harmony. This is the same need pointed out by Scruton: our 'need to live in harmony with others'. The problem is, how?

We should recognize that people won't give up rights, since they won't give up boundaries. And this may be the beginning of the solution. As concepts, rights and boundaries are interdependent: every right is constituted by the boundary that protects it. My right to play requires a designated area to play in. My right to express my mind requires a platform where I can be heard. To divorce rights from their protecting boundaries is to turn them in the direction of abuse and aggression – such we know from social media, where the right to free expression has become the plague of cyberbullying, trolling and witch-hunting. So, where there are rights, there must also be order.

Islamic law sets a useful precedent here. In a public space, it is not individuals whose rights are a priority, but the space itself. This right is termed 'the street right', implying the precedence of the common good over any personal benefit. The Islamic 'street right' looks at each individual space as a private sphere that should be respected and protected from violation: this is termed *hurumat*, the respect for sacred things. Hence, sitting in public roads is discouraged, and the street requires you to greet those who greet you, to refrain from any type of harm, to promote virtue and prevent vice. These simple requirements create conditions for active social participation without transgressing private boundaries. There is a balancing act here: we risk either a complete loss of boundaries, as in Samanani's Kilburn neighbourhood, or (in fact mostly 'and') a negative avoidance of others and a total retreat from the public sphere.

Another instructive example is the European allotment system, which allows people to come together to cultivate a piece of public land. As well as being an active way of creating a common good, this creates space for negotiation and collaboration. During the years of war in my city of Homs, many people were imprisoned in their apartments for over two years. In one newly developed housing block, the few remaining families had to create a community in their collective attempt to survive. The men had no jobs to go to and plenty of spare time. They looked at the area surrounding their building, which was like all the ground around such blocks:

a swirling wasteland of dust and plastic bags. And they turned this piece of land into an allotment project. They began by growing tomatoes and lettuce, then corn, sunflowers, beans and herbs. In the back corner there was room for a shed for chickens, so fresh eggs arrived, to be distributed among the neighbours. Soon there was evening coffee for women in the garden (when the shelling seemed far away) while the men played cards close by.

In order for there to be a common good there must be a society, which in turn must be built like Bachelard's house, so as to embody a 'hierarchy of the various functions of inhabiting'. Naturally, this social hierarchy of functions requires a standard of evaluation, whether it be wealth, family, status or class. However – unlike the empty entitlement of class – production and social contribution are genuine features of the common good. Exchange is essentially trade, and trade depends on production and requires compromise and negotiation. So exchange has not only a visual aspect, the aggregation of people in a place and the activities they display, as Lynch touches upon; nor only a technical aspect, the arrangement and look of buildings where activities take place, as referred to by Jacobs – it also has a *moral* aspect, which is to a large extent a condition of its permanence.

The more it targets the common good, the more *ethical* trade becomes. A commonly used meaning of the term 'ethical trade' relates to paying decent prices to producers in developing countries, avoiding packaging or manufacturing techniques that damage the environment, and so on. But all of these are responses to the Factory model. When I think of truly ethical trade, I am considering from a different angle how trade can be undertaken in an ethical way.

Ethical trade in my view is an entirely different phenomenon from the Factory City model, in which trade hovers over the heads of people: mass-produced, exploitative of their energies and resources and captured for the benefit of the few. Truly ethical trade, by contrast, is distributed from the bottom up and spread over multiple players in society. It creates conditions in which small businesses and crafts can thrive and allows for diversification that will inevitably beget negotiation, compromise and a genuine embrace of 'the other'. Social cohesion is organically established through social and economic structures that demand the manners and courtesies referred to by Scruton, which soften the city's boundaries. Thus does ethical trade establish trust – a trust that is *earned* in a daily testing of boundaries among people who, in this way, work for the common good.

Of course, this implies that there will also be a tension between private benefit and the common good, between the proximity needed to acknowledge the other and the need for privacy. Hence we also need to make the right choices, and there is an opening here to corruption. Like name tags, buildings carry the identity of their occupants. The look, size and location of a building give a sense of its place within the urban fabric: a private company won't open its headquarters in an area where streets are too narrow for high-speed traffic, with no room for private parking, or if the property is too small for the development of office space. Unless collectively purchased and razed to the ground, urban areas can point towards certain uses and continue to do so as they age (a process I will discuss in more depth later in this book). Social cohesion exists because of a meaningful and moral intention of settlement, which in turn expresses itself in the organization and appearance of buildings, which in turn promote a sustained social identity. This healthy cycle of input and feedback can be disrupted at either end: the morality of the social fabric, or the aesthetics of the urban fabric. Our examination of boundaries in this chapter is one way of looking at this process. Home involves achieving the right balance between those two elements: finding the anchor that secures us in life's sea of uncertainties.

Many of us have lost our homes in this sea; yet, inside us, there remains a secret 'black box' in which the original image of home is locked away. Home, where we feel safe and secure like a child in that oneiric house, firmly rooted in the ground but with a capacious opening towards the sky. We wrap this image in meaning and we reach for the key to the cherished box every time we feel threatened in the great big world, considering ourselves very lucky if the key actually matches the lock of our real front door. Those whose places have not provided them with this primary image of home (such as the refugee children I met in Melbourne; but also many of today's 'global citizens') lose something fundamental to their well-being.

Somewhere in the air between Berlin and Beirut, a Lebanese passenger sitting beside me confided that, after living for almost thirty years in Germany, she is still unsure 'where home is'. It felt as if she were reaching for that key. Lebanon is a sacked place, a place of social, economic and political collapse. Yet, my companion told me, she still glances over her shoulder as she drives on highways through the German landscape, looking for the sea of Beirut.

Living by the water had marked this lady's existence, as it does for many people who have experienced life beside this particularly treacherous source of abundance. In Arabic culture, the sea is described colloquially as treacherous, mainly because it is unknown. It appears limitless, deep and dark; it changes mood unexpectedly. But it is loved for its abundance. Sailors, fishermen, and even sea sport adventurers learn to navigate the unpredictability of the sea by respecting it.

In Beirut today, however, little – if anything – is respected. The recent explosion of its harbour area seems like nothing more than a bubble of the boiling pot on which the entire city sits. For many, it was the final straw.

Prior to the destruction, entering the city from the north, you would have encountered David Adjaye's enormous Aishti department store in its swollen red cage, bluntly blocking the waterfront. From there you could catch only a glimpse or two of the sea behind a forbidding line of big stores and fancy restaurants until you reached the Rawshe Rock, where the coast road is elevated, though offering only a high-nose look at the almost entirely subsided and built-up coastline. My Lebanese–German friend has lost her home; the turquoise horizon of the Mediterranean can live for her only in that secret box.

After Beirut fell victim to civil war and warlords, the city was rebuilt according to the whims and interests of those who had led the war against each other in times of conflict. In peacetime, they led a war against the city. Private companies rule the city, while immigration money fuels its engines. It suffers from endless problems: lack of governance, jammed traffic, poor amenities, high pollution, social hostility, urban segregation, you name it. But something really stands out, which is that it is impossible to walk through. As a port city it has grown lengthwise, parallel to the coast. During post-war reconstruction the city lost its centre, which became the 'downtown' shopping destination for rich visitors from other countries. Disconnected from the sea by a coastal highway, the boundary of the city begins with a forbidding seafront which is echoed in parallel main roads towards the inner parts of the town. This horizontal grid is pierced with a forest of newly built high-rises, filling the islands between the traffic. There is no space for pavements: instead there are interrupted ultra-thin strips that rarely connect for more than a few blocks before being disconnected by features related to the movement of vehicles. Moreover, the network of roads is built with little consideration for the city's topography, which is hilly in some parts and sloping towards the coast in others. So the roads are elevated in between the islands of buildings that face the sea line, in a race to get a glimpse of the blue horizon.

In the midst of all this, crossing the road makes no sense: you risk your life only to reach an endless fenced strip of abandoned pavement, brushed by a lonely worker with a broom. The elevated road holds no cross-connection to the row of buildings one level down and offers no exits from its horizontal trap. Sectarian segregation in

David Adjaye's Aishti department store in Beirut.

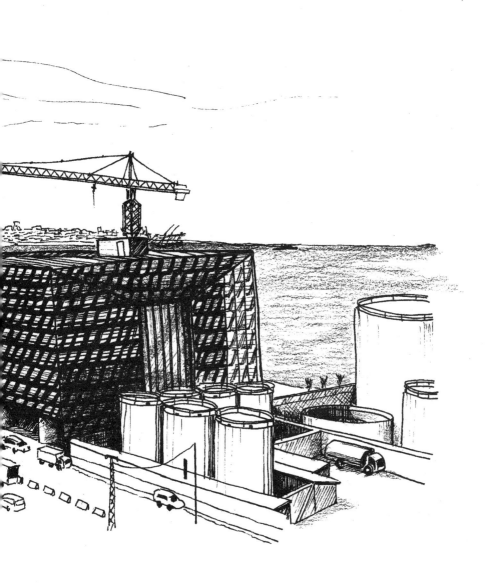

a city like Beirut is overshadowed by the lack of generosity of the city and the no-exit appearance it offers its visitors. Instead of aromas of nature and food, you get charred smoke in your nostrils. Instead of trees, you're overshadowed by concrete giants. And instead of doors you're rejected by sealed apartments and private security guards. People are angry all the time, stuck in traffic in this built wasteland. Glaring glass cubes and blurry reflections of a trapped life inside high-end businesses and modern galleries are the mark of a city that has kicked out its residents and replaced them with bank loans.

Beirut is an extreme example of everything that can go wrong in the cities of our colonized, modernized and globalized world. At the other end of the spectrum is a city that amassed its wealth by enslaving colonized people and trading in tobacco, and which is now a leading production and trade centre for aviation, cars and spirits. Bristol – the city of Burke, Brunel and Banksy – is, like Beirut, a hilly port city. However, it is entirely different from Beirut when it comes to the planning and management of space. You quickly discover this when walking around the city: different areas are connected in different places, as the network of roads allows you to reach your destination from various starting points involving similar distances. Furthermore, the city manages its hilly nature beautifully, keeping a balance between the built and the grown. Unlike Beirut's dried-up river, the river Avon in Bristol is kept alive, with terraced housing on its banks and no barriers between the passers-by and the inhabitants. Whether you are making your way through the cluster of single houses with their rose-dotted gardens, or beside the attached blocks with their double-fronted stairs, as a passer-by you're allowed to penetrate the edge of this private realm without disturbing it. The stairs in front of the housing lead to an elevated terrace next to the river's bank, so you don't get stuck at the edge of water, yet you're within touching distance of the river. The same is true in different corners of the city. Doors that open to courtyards, arches that frame shortcuts to back streets, stairs that lead down a bridge, a dock or a highway; no matter where your feet lead you, you find an exit.

I was invited to take part in an event in Bristol. The organizers had prepared an exciting way for participants to explore the city by developing a book of themed walking tours: Commerce and Public Life, Romanticism, Art and Culture, Nature, The University, and Brunel. We set out in the pouring rain and my guide map soon began falling to pieces under the thick ropes of water. Yet I had little difficulty finding my way by following the topology of the city, which flowed seamlessly with the road network. My steps sometimes diverted into little corners of private gardens whose beauty extended to the public space of the road, with no sharp distinction between

Victorian terraced houses, Cliftonwood, Bristol, seen across the River Avon.

the two. I found these qualities very refreshing, even if the whole experience was rather wet!

Bristol is not without its problems, of course, and I have only experienced a flying visit to the city. However, I was struck by what seemed to work so well in the areas I saw: namely their connectivity and their elegance. Elsewhere, despite the city's efforts to conceal it, homelessness and division are painfully evident. One can easily detect this by slipping off the edges of the well-looked-after neighbourhoods or even just by walking after sunset – two decisions I almost had cause to regret. Indeed, the same two phenomena, homelessness and division, are among the disgraces that wealthy Western cities typically try to sweep under the carpet by offering their visitors a semblance of order. They are a consequence of placing city and town centres at the mercy of global business: undermining local resources in order to enable international corporations to take root and flourish. But they are also part of the chain of events that this book tries to narrate: the Factory City was one episode, but there is much more to explore. Our examination of boundaries is an important aspect of understanding what has happened in both the city and the countryside, where the people have left home and home has left the people.

In a poem simply titled 'Damascus', the late Palestinian poet Mahmoud Darwish describes this enchanting city:

> *In Damascus sleeps the stranger on his shadow while standing,*
> *Like a minaret in the bed of eternity,*
> *He doesn't yearn for anyone,*
> *Nor for any place.*

How does the stranger 'sleep on his shadow while standing'; why does he do that, how can he do that? Well, because in Damascus this stranger fears no treachery. He feels safe in this spiritual place, like the ancient minarets marking the continuity of a place that became home. Although Damascus does create this impression on her visitors, often giving rise to an indelible haze of emotions, it is also true that this place, the oldest continuously inhabited city in the world, has been gradually losing its charm. The story of its decline begins in the 18th and 19th centuries, and is discussed in Linda Schatkowski Schilcher's book *Families in Politics: Damascene Factions and Estates of the 18th and 19th Centuries* (1985). Schilcher chose to explore those deeply turbulent times in the life of the region from the perspective of the role of the notable families in politics who ruled Damascus and the region under the Ottomans. Syria at this time was called Greater Syria, before being divided by the Sykes–Picot accord after the fall of the Ottoman Empire.

Greater Syria, or the Levant, was a land bordered to the east by the coast of the Mediterranean, to the west by Iraq. The mountain chain of Anatolia (Turkey today) marked its north, while the desert of the Hijaz (currently Saudi) bordered the south. For administrative purposes Greater Syria was divided into four provinces, each with a governor ruling under orders from the Sultanate: in the north the province of Aleppo, in the coastal regions those of Tripoli and Sidon, and the rest in the province of Damascus.

The social, economic and political changes that took place during the 18th and 19th centuries set the course for the events that followed, leading to the endless conflicts and wars we see today. But aside from their historical importance, the social dynamics of this transformative period could well explain what seems to be a mystery in the eyes of the world today: why do people in the Middle East kill each other? This type of killing is an act of highest treachery that is dubbed 'civil war'; it involves not only a total loss of home, but the literal destruction of it.

The 18th and 19th centuries, as well as being a time of industrial revolution, were a period when foreign powers had their arms dipped to the elbows in the internal life of Syrian society and politics, under the shaky house of Ottoman rule and its foggy leadership. Schilcher outlines the urban configuration of Damascus in those two critical centuries as an enclosed city behind a wall, together with surrounding areas of the Ottoman province. The city managed self-sufficiency by depending on what Schilcher calls the 'inner ring of supply' (the city inside the wall and the surrounding land adjacent to it), and the 'outer ring of supply' (the agricultural lands stretching to the open fields of Homs and Hama to the north, and to the lands of Houran to the south). More interestingly, she classifies the inner city inside the wall and close by into three main urban areas.

First is the 'central rectangle', based on the Roman planning grid with its two main perpendicular roads, inside which lie the Great Umayyad Mosque, the main souk, the religious schools and colleges (madrassas), and the residences of the merchants and those working in the souk. Alongside this, to the west, is 'the Ottoman area', where government and administrative buildings and centres lie and recreational areas are situated. Finally, to the south is the so-called 'local area', where local goods, food and production tools are made and locally exchanged.

The first time I saw the Khan al-Azm, I wondered why such a magnificent jewel would be buried under the dust of official neglect and public uninterest. Feeling the same awe that had filled me on visiting the Al-Azm palaces in Damascus and in Hama, I wondered why this family which built such wondrous structures had no memorial – not even a statue of one of its 'heroes'. The only reputation that its descendants enjoy today is that they are posh, wealthy and many of them live abroad. This made me question Syrian society: is it an ungrateful one? Or could it be related to censorship? Is there some historical stigma that we wish to brush under the carpet?

No fewer than nine rulers of Damascus during the period 1725–1808 were members of the Al-Azm family. Their dynasty gained the trust of the Ottoman Empire's central government by fulfilling the mission entrusted to them of protecting pilgrimage convoys to Mecca from raids by nomads. Internally, they had to suppress any rebellion and soothe public resentment of the Ottoman policies of taxation and military recruiting. For this they were generously rewarded by full control over prices and routes for the grain trade. Their rule marked the beginning of a significant social change: in order to serve their own economic interests, the family ruled by *'asabiyya*. They guarded their positions with marital connections throughout Damascene society. Moreover, they allied themselves on the one hand with Sufism and on the other with the military. Sufism is supposed to be an individual road towards self-discipline and faith, but it quickly turned into a religious apprenticeship in which students sit at the feet of their superiors and remake the religious way of life as an intellectual adventure. This trend especially flourished under late Ottoman rule and was easily twisted into cult practices and mysticism. Meanwhile, marital networking laid the foundations for a long and devious rule. These strategic manipulations enabled the Al-Azm family to control the market and to corner any challengers to their authority in the southern 'local area' of Al-Meedan.

Al-Meedan was the area where trade occurred with the countryside and the nomads, allowing, as with the example of Homs's souk described in Chapter 2, the development of urban interaction. As Schilcher explains, it was a busy area with a relatively well-developed infrastructure; over time, as it expanded, its importance rivalled that of the central rectangle. 'Although it cannot be considered by any standard a poor or underdeveloped area, yet the big size and nature of its trade activity, and the great number of peasants and Bedouin who visited its stores, shops, coffee shops, and public baths, in addition to the military groups who lacked discipline to a certain extent created an atmosphere of turbulence and riot.'[23]

In the 1740s, Assad Pasha (who left us the Khan al-Azm and the Azm Palace) transformed the economy of Damascus by launching an attack on Al-Meedan. His intention was to squelch the rising opposition of lower- and middle-class traders in the south. Assad Pasha's troops blighted Al-Meedan, burning and looting hundreds of houses, arresting and murdering opposition supporters.[24] The effect of this was not only to disconcert his opponents but to establish a new economic order in which the Al-Azm family were the sole dictators of the market. They steered Damascus into their lands in the Syrian north and the west, up towards Hama and into Lebanon's mountains. Higher-quality grain from the south was prevented from reaching the souk. Moreover, by superseding Al-Meedan's traders, the Al-Azm family became the sole buyers of the south's grains and the market's main purveyor, dictating terms, quantities and prices.

In short, the Al-Azm replaced a social order based on vocation with one based on ʿasabiyya. They manipulated key figures and families across different classes and economic categories, stratifying Damascene society according to the rules of their game. In a sense, they established themselves as a *tribe*, ruling a great city during a time of decline and chaos. In their suppression of Al-Meedan and its localism, they pushed the city's boundaries towards globalization. Nineteenth-century Damascus was quickly turned into a Factory City, which took no time to explode. This explosion was very similar to the current one that Syria is witnessing. Both eruptions followed a similar chain of events – economic orientation, foreign intervention and manipulation of boundaries – and both were misinterpreted as 'civil war'.

So we are back to the question: why do people in the Middle East kill each other? The usual answer given by the Western media and experts' reports is: sectarianism. Well, sectarianism is definitely a symptom; but is it really the *cause*? I believe that sectarian divides result in part from economic causes, but are also exacerbated by the systematic undermining of three main factors that contribute to the creation of a home: religion, production and the built environment.

The 1860s saw the beginning of the end of the Ottoman Empire, but also the end of the rule of the Al-Azm and their ʿasabiyya. They were persecuted by the Ottoman government for failing to anticipate and contain the events that were alarmingly described as the first Syrian civil war. (As in those times – and with much less hesitation than Syrians themselves – Western commentators today analyse the current conflict in Syria in sectarian terms, and therefore as a plain case of a second civil war. I don't find it hard to accept this term, but only if it is understood as describing the consequences of the events rather than their roots.)

The decline of the Ottoman Empire in the 19th century was the gate through which Western countries managed to guarantee their commercial and strategic interests, dividing the Levant between opposing powers.[25] In the 1840s, the middle core of today's Lebanon (Mount Lebanon) had witnessed growing tensions between different ethnoreligious groups, the Christian Maronites and the Druze, in that part of Greater Syria. Under pressure from Western powers, the land was divided into two districts subordinate to the feeble Sultanate: one for the Maronites in the north (to be supported by the French) and one for the Druze in the south (to be supported by the British). This division wasn't only one of geography but of economics and social class, between the Druze as feudal landlords and the peasant Maronites. The road between Damascus and Beirut marked the border between the districts.

This Western-imposed division exacerbated social and economic pressures, leading to a rebellion among the Maronites: the so-called Revolution of Keserwan. This conflict resulted not only in horrific crimes, but also in the devastation of the silk crops.[26] The result was a complete destruction of the silk industry in the whole of Greater Syria, followed by general impoverishment and a further inflammation of the conflict. The ground for this had been prepared for a long time, as foreign missionaries had flooded into the region under the cover of religion. Who can argue against building new churches, schools and cultural centres? But in reality, the new schools were aiming to teach foreign languages and create rival loyalties to those that had grown indigenously. The incoming missionaries were, in effect, dividing up economic opportunities and power networks by religion – their own religion being the privileged one.

A similar story took place in Damascus, where the trade in grains and textiles was subject to manipulation by foreign powers. The British and the French vied to pull this rug from under each other during the Napoleonic Wars. Through their missionaries they granted special treatment to their affiliates in the region, facilitating those who did business with Europe through long-term loans, easy access to credit, and special positions.

In those times of political collapse, missionaries and their cultural affiliates opened the door for their converts to privileges that were hard to obtain by other means. (Hence people from other sects, such as Orthodox Christians, started converting to Catholicism, which was beginning to be perceived as a 'concubine sect' on account of its economic affiliations with the West.) This dynamic was not new; it had existed since the early days of foreign intervention in the declining Ottoman Empire. The trick was to apply pressure, while creating the terms that required just such pressure to be maintained. It was a strategy that facilitated the penetration of foreign interests into the body of Syrian society, through the development of 'special' commercial relationships with the Christians and Jews of Greater Syria. Loyal subjects who mastered Western languages and modern skills were rewarded with positions as translators and commercial representatives for the Americans and Europeans residing on the shores of Lebanon, from where they could 'protect their interests' while keeping an eye on 'minority rights'. For such a noble purpose, the foreign masters granted nationality and diplomatic immunity to their indigenous servants.

Moreover, the policy of doing business with Europe put pressure on the weak Ottoman government to make advantageous deals – for example, granting substantial tariff cuts to the British in 1838 and unjustly promoting European merchandise over local products. In this way English cotton replaced Syrian flax and found its monopolized way into the European-leveraged looms of the Christian Catholics in Damascus. Schilcher mentions a legal case raised by Muslim merchants in Damascus against their neighbours in the Catholic quarter; it led nowhere, since the European argument of 'protecting minorities' rights' was used to justify a foreign-imposed monopoly.[27] In a conservative Muslim society, dealing in credit is prohibited by religion, but doing business with Europe at that time meant that a credit system had to be created. Inevitably this was mostly controlled by Christians and Jews, who became the main creditors to the whole market.

In another parallel with the events of today, you might hear of the massacres of Christians in Syria in the 1860s, but you would be less likely to hear about the contexts in which such horrible crimes were committed, who was behind them and who challenged them; how the bloodshed was stopped, or at what cost. Like the conflict today, this situation was characterized as a Syrian civil war. And, like today, people blamed the problem on its effects rather than its cause.

Riots between the Maronites and the Druze in Mount Lebanon eventually spread into Damascus. But what appeared to be religiously motivated violence was really a consequence of economic imbalance, itself the result of social injustice and social isolation. From Beirut, the needle eye through which foreign power initially crept in, the thread was pulled into the textile industry of the inner cities. During this period Europe was experiencing a sequence of recessions,[28] while local Syrian markets were being affected by the import of cheap foreign goods. The silk workshops were declining along with their local outlets while the privileged sects kept their strength, feeding off their relationships with foreign protectors. (Sometimes literally: in the 1860s grain famine, French missionaries distributed bread and grain to Christian Syrians with no reports of equivalent philanthropy towards the hungry Muslims.)[29]

In Beirut, the region's first bank was opened in 1857: a British institution called the Sultanate's Ottoman Bank, which facilitated business with Europe. French factories for the silk industry were opened in Lebanon using Syrian silk thread, though the factory, the workers and the market were all French. Britain soon followed in France's footsteps.[30] Eventually both the grain trade and the silk craft were monopolized, and the main profiteers were foreign affiliates. The land then became endangered, because impoverished people began selling off their properties. This was the point of no return: both the craft and the land had fallen into the hands of outsiders. There can be no rise after such a fall, for a self-sustaining economy is impossible without its main ingredients: knowledge and place. Hence, there will be no home.

Simmering on that fire, Syria was left in suspense while the riots raged. Once the violence reached Damascus, the Catholic quarter was plundered and burnt with the loss of many innocent lives. After that, events moved quickly towards collapse. The Ottoman authorities, in a desperate attempt to regain control, organized mass arrests and public executions, but to no avail; the foreign powers had found their long-awaited excuse to enter in force.[31] Soon Greater Syria had fallen and been occupied, divided and devastated.

To understand the real consequences of these events, a closer look into how they were reported in overseas newspapers such as the *New York Times* can be of help. While focusing on conflict between the Christians and the Druze, these reports largely overlook the role of the Bedouin. It is important to know that the Bedouin helped in the massacres. By the nature of their way of life they had no homes to lose, and hence could be hired as militia to carry out crimes against settled people and their property, as their recruiters required. As discussed earlier, the Bedouin were the main reason why cities in the Levant were protected by walls, and commercial relationships with them have a history that reflects their nomadic and unattached character.

Another important fact is the locus of the fight, in the city of Damascus. The attacks on Christians that took place in the 1860s were not random; nor were all the Christians of the city attacked. Specifically, the horrors of plunder and killing took place in what had become a Catholic quarter of the old city of Damascus, which thanks to foreign penetration had become a self-contained, independently enriched and isolated place. Other Christians (mostly Orthodox) who were living among their Muslim neighbours were protected and saved. And those who committed the crimes weren't from just any random parts of the city; they were from the poorest, most derelict neighbourhoods. This reflects the economic causes on the one hand, and the connected role of urbanism on the other.

We must consider, too, that thousands of Christian families had taken refuge under the protection of Abd Al-Qadir Al-Jazairei at his citadel,[32] while Muslim families in the city offered sanctuary to their frightened Christian neighbours. This was not because they were less faithful, or 'moderate' in today's terminology, but because all of them, Muslim and Christian, stood by what their religions command them to do, which is to treat their neighbours with compassion.

All of this is still highly relevant to the Syrian war's current reality. While foreign powers were declaring that it had become impossible for Christians to continue living in a country like 1860s Syria, the reality proved them wrong. The Muslim-majority society in cooperation with minorities from other religions was able to heal – if not completely – despite everything that could have prevented it achieving this. The Christians continued to live door to door and church to mosque with their Muslim neighbours. But their cities were changing beyond their control. Syria as a country was moving into a continuous decline despite the resistance of its society, which explains the mismatch between its brittle surface and the flexibility and adaptability of the once settled communities beneath it.

That trajectory of decline continued with the decision of the International Convention (an alliance of Austria, Great Britain, France, Prussia and Russia, many of whose consulates were attacked during the riots) to 'investigate' the crimes of the 1860s and dispatch their troops to re-establish order. Although it was clear that the division of Lebanon in 1842 – a division they had made way for – was the main reason for the escalation of events leading to the civil war, the resolution of the committee was to further divide the region. This led to the isolation of Lebanon as a Christian territory, with an assigned tribal system of sects to 'rule' it, from 1861. Then came the Sykes–Picot accord, and the French mandate – and with the mandate came modern, 'rational' town planning. This has shaped our cities and societies into conflicting tribes and a new kind of nomadism, ruled by 'asabiyya and perpetuated by the rigid boundaries of architecture that has been cleansed of the qualities that constitute home.

Today, things remain very much the same. The West still regards our region as one of great chaos, elements of which need to be sorted as if into different Tupperware boxes. Unfortunately, the more categorization there is, the further we move away from any real solution. Even 'inclusiveness' is approached by tossing in 'one of each': the big salad bowl.

Furthermore, attacks on specific communities and on the social fabric continue, with the same capitalist approach adopted by the Al-Azm family and with the open market economy the French and the British deployed in their favour. The attack launched by the Al-Azm against the Al-Meedan has evolved into an eruption in boundaries, making possible the European manipulation of the newly established 'asabiyya. But there is still an underlying stratum beneath the surface of events; the Al-Meedan episode proved to be the starting point from which transformations of both the city and the surrounding Syrian countryside began. Damascus, formerly a self-sufficient city surrounded by lush orchards and widespread crops, lost its autarkic economy. The great capital wasn't alone in this: in 1875, the Ottoman government announced its bankruptcy. Many people, in response, decided it was time to flee the sinking ship.

Human migration, generally speaking, tends to stick to a beaten track. Mostly, people move from the small and contained towards the big and liberating – from the limited to the unlimited. And here lies the dilemma: finding abundance is conditional on breaking free of limitations, the very break that leaves us exposed to treachery. In a binary confrontation, man must choose between the convenience of abundance and the safety of confinement; the two cannot be combined. There is no better example of such a trade-off than the one made in rural areas that surround cities. Aesop's fable 'The Town Mouse and the Country Mouse' makes exactly this point, presenting a choice between 'security and opulence' – between the safety of the non-treacherous countryside, and the abundance and convenience of the city.

In travelling from the ploughed womb of the rural towards the stretched horizons of the urban, people are no longer at the mercy of nature – instead they find themselves at the mercy of money. For anyone wishing to swap the monotony of the rhythmic seasons for the fluctuating beat of markets, that is the necessary price to be paid. In pursuit of big dreams, many people cling to the ropes of sailing ships following the image of a prosperous shore; a picture of an independent family house is hanging on the wall of the imagination, waiting for the city to set it free.

Back in the small town or remote village, the green grass is for cattle. The land demands many sacrifices; it takes up your time, your sweat and your mind. Life can be arduous – cold is too cold, hot is too hot. The sky is your omen, so you learn how to read its colours, clouds and wind. The seeds you sow and the crops you harvest draw your daily plans. Depending on them, time can run short or stretch out endlessly; life can be very good or it can go very wrong – but you can't read that on a stock market screen. You must learn to live it, in the absence of control. In a rural community you also learn to appreciate the simple and the small, to be content with little, to be patient and diligent. But it isn't this way all the time: nature can be generous, and when it gives, it offers abundance in the form of food to eat and crops to exchange.

Until the recent past, people in the countryside understood this balance of pros and cons. That is why, despite constant migration towards the city, the village was never abandoned as it is in danger of being today. The balance between the rural and the urban was not in the past sabotaged so severely as it has recently been. It is estimated that by the year 2050, 75 percent of the world's population will inhabit cities; this means we no longer live in an equilibrium that would guarantee the well-being of both city and village. Fear of starvation and widespread famine are linked to climate change, but not enough consideration is given to the element of one-way migration. Even allowing for some people's decision to live in rural areas while maintaining work connections with the city, the abandonment of agriculture as a settlement mode in the village is on the rise. So why are people increasingly abandoning the countryside and its mode of living, and what does that mean for both the city and the village?

In order to understand home, all modes of human settlement should be explored. I am reminded here of Ibn Khaldoun's note that 'urbanism is the ultimate aim and goal of the nomad'.[33] Both rural and urban settlement offer a home, an alternative to the roaming that is the condition of the nomad – yet the trajectory of movement continues to proceed from village to city. Why does the village fail more frequently to be *home* than the city, and at what cost to both?

All over the world, the Factory City of the 20th century marked the beginning of a radical shift of migration from country to city. One man who took an early look at the causes of what was then, in America, called 'the rural social problem' was Charles Josiah Galpin, whose book *Rural Life* was published in 1918. Galpin was an agricultural economist who developed the first clear sociological definition of the rural communities surrounding a central village.[34] He offered invaluable insights into the rural mindset of his time.

The 'problem' in question was a lack of social organization, which undermined political and economic progress. Galpin was writing on a turning page in time, at the beginning of great technological advances in communication (the telephone and the automobile) and the prime time of industrialization. He was fully aware of their effects, and his analysis distinguished between what he called the 'hoe-farmer', or peasant, and the 'machine-farmer', or farm engineer.[35] The difference is set out in terms of the labour a farmer undertakes. Galpin lists different categories of 'influences': physiographic, residential, occupational, institutional and urban. Through these, he differentiates between the urban and rural psyche.

One of these influences stands out in Galpin's wide-ranging discussion: gravity. In observing the daily labour of the 'primitive farmer', which includes all sorts of 'lifting and carrying', gravity emerges as a force that shapes rural thinking and social organization – simply because farmers are constantly working to overcome it. They are also in conflict with the climate – a force from which the urbanite, constantly sheltered under his roof, has become quite 'independent'.[36]

Ibn Khaldoun also considered nature and vocation as essential elements in understanding social life and consequently settlement. This, for our purposes, is necessary in order to understand the *shape* of settlement and how it is to be built. In that context, Galpin offers 'soil' as an 'influence' that combines both nature and vocation in rural life. The farmer's work revolves around the soil, which is also a source of prejudice against him: urban dwellers, Galpin suggests, associate workers on the land with dirt and grime, regarding them as vulgar rather than as noble inhabitants of the wide open spaces.[37]

The nature of agriculture as an act of managed reproduction involves farmers in 'dealing with parentage, lineage, individual differences'.[38] It also forces them to recognize limitations to their control and 'accept the behavior of seed, plant, and animal'.[39] There is the farmer, working with the moods of nature in humility and respect, pulled down by gravity and lifted up by the wind. For whole seasons, he waits patiently for the very soil that diminishes his status among men to unwrap heaven's gift. Unlike the urbanite who lives in Bachelard's oneiric house, 'dual polarity' for the farmer has no framework of boundaries. He is the vertical centrality; he stands between earth and sky without barriers. No wonder Galpin's analysis of the rural mind found farmers to be 'sovereign, animistic, individualistic, conservative, and above all, men'.[40]

Galpin shines a light on the farmer's lack of control over his product, which is really the product of nature – the creation of God, not man. This is what 'marks the difference between the farmer and the industrial worker'.[41] As he puts it: 'Broadly speaking, the urban worker works with people, for people, and upon the minds of people, whatever else he may do; while the farmer, living detached from people, works neither with people, nor for people, nor upon people.'[42]

Galpin's aim was essentially to mass produce the countryside; in a sense, to turn the village into a Factory Village. He wanted to organize the American farming business, transform it into an industry. And he succeeded. His suggestion of creating a central village around which satellite villages gather shares characteristics with early examples of regional planning as we know it today. Using this concept, he coined the term 'rurban', referring to the intertwining of city and village through the transformation of their respective social and economic circumstances.

It must be noted that the American farmer was, before Galpin's ideas took hold, extremely isolated compared to farmers in countries where space is more compact and human contact more frequent – so in a sense, his quest to create a more connected countryside was a benign one. Nonetheless, he was aware of the risk he was putting on his bet in automating farming. He recognized that the centralization and organization required by automation would probably affect the rural character, leading to a divorce between the mentality of the farmer and his product; and that forcing farming to sacrifice its unique qualities might very well annul it altogether. And he was right in that as well. We see Galpin's rurbanization all over the world today: the city is no longer a city, just as the village is no longer a village. All has become rurban. Agriculture has become agribusiness, and the life of the countryside is managed by offices in the town.

In this light, Al-Azm's suppression of Al-Meedan in the 19th century might now be understood as an assault on a city boundary that offered osmosis with the countryside without collapsing into rurbanism. Urban areas like Al-Meedan, or the souk in Homs, represented fault lines that were permeable enough to keep the flow of business going between city and village, but at the same time resilient enough to maintain the distinctive characteristics of living inherent to both places. The importance of this clarity regarding boundaries, for both the city and the village, is that it is the only way either of them can keep their social fabric intact. Whether in America, in Syria or anywhere else in the world, the disruption of boundaries that was initiated by the Factory City led to the need for a Factory Village. The melting pot which dissolved all boundaries and turned cities and villages into rurban areas, spreading without control in every direction, can accept all charges for the treacherous crime of engendering social conflict.

4
THE FEAR OF LONELINESS
Achieving Acceptance

Looking Backward: the words imply a nostalgic, regretful view of the past. In fact they are the title of an idealistic novel of the future, published in 1888. A science-fiction bestseller of its time, this work by Edward Bellamy imagines a utopian society in the year 2000. It tells the story of Julian West, a young American who wakes up after a hypnosis-induced sleep lasting 113 years. Through West's dialogue with supporting characters who introduce him to the accomplishments and advances of the idealistic new age, Bellamy lays out his vision for a utopian future in what is effectively a 470-page socialist manifesto.

At a time when economic and social depression and recession were sweeping across America and Europe, the springing up of hundreds of 'Bellamy Clubs' wasn't the only response to this novel. It also left its mark on the pages of other socialist writings, and influenced the intellectual and political movements of its day.

Bellamy's dream was of a nationally owned US manufacturing sector, with goods equally distributed among all citizens. It inspired Marxist revolutionaries, socialist visionaries and romantic medievalists. It also spurred on one of the most influential movements in the history of urban planning: the Garden City movement. Inspired by *Looking Backward*, English urban planner Ebenezer Howard wrote his *To-morrow: A Peaceful Path to Real Reform* (1898); four years later, it was reissued as *Garden Cities of To-morrow*.

The principle of the Garden City is apparent in its name: an attempt to reconcile country with city. But as the name also reveals, nature in this context is somewhat trimmed and polished: the 'dirty' soil about which Galpin would later write is cleansed by the suburban life of the upgraded blue-collar worker. It is a 'garden', not a 'farm', and it's a 'city', not a 'town'. As imagined by Howard, it combines the best of both worlds: the opulence of the city and the security of the countryside. Howard sought to overcome two main problems: the crowdedness and uncontrolled sprawl of the city, where pollution and property prices were both too high, and the lack of activity and progressiveness in the monotonous but clean and beautiful countryside.

Much like Galpin's system of village planning, Howard's Garden City would be one of several satellite cities, connected radially with the help of railways to a larger central city. The outer boundaries of each city would be surrounded by a green belt. Once the central city reached saturation point in terms of people and businesses there would be no need for it to expand further, as a new neighbouring centre of activity would take in the excess. Garden Cities would be divided into residential boulevards, central parks and services, with peripheral rings of industrial activity and railway connectivity. But the *Looking Backward* socialist dream couldn't be completed without finding the shared resources to fund this ambitious project. Howard initially proposed a 'cooperative commonwealth', in which the community would share ownership of land and benefit collectively from rising property values.[1]

But when the first Garden Cities were developed in England and America, it proved impossible to keep house prices affordable for blue-collar workers. Most of the population of Letchworth Garden City in Hertfordshire, England, were skilled middle-class workers, while in Radburn, New Jersey, isolation and crime eventually turned it into the antithesis of what Howard had intended to create.

Even so, the Garden City concept retained its appeal to urban planners for many decades, leading to the creation of numerous examples around the world. Most of these have since become 'dormitory suburbs', again falling short of Howard's utopian ideal. The dormitory suburb or garden suburb excludes the productive aspect and resident working class of the Garden City, keeping only the shell of it for its new residents: housing for the wealthy, with a peripheral location on the outskirts of cities to which the residents commute by car. In short, the Garden City was hijacked by exactly the type of set-up Howard was hoping to avoid. It became a haven for rich people who wanted to escape the urban grind, while urbanization took the direction of what one of Howard's contemporaries, the Scottish planner Patrick Geddes, called the 'conurbation': a term referring to the growth and merging of urban areas into a single region of merged labour markets and transportation networks.

Galpin had tried to pull the village closer to the city and Howard to do the opposite, but in Geddes's conurbation the two collided and merged to form a kaleidoscope of the original human activities: agriculture and trade. Industrialization transformed both centres of agriculture and centres of trade, absorbing them into the modern service economy.

What remains of the Garden City movement is hardly related to its original tenets. The question is why? I believe the answer lies in the way Howard designed the property ownership system. His original vision of a cooperative commonwealth was compromised by the realities of financing; instead, each Garden City was owned by a private corporation that built and managed its property. The city was preplanned and predivided; its production engines needed only a push on the start button. The fact that people had no free rein over their living arrangements was, in my view, the Achilles' heel of the Garden City movement.

Human settlement is a group effort because humans fear loneliness. We need others – not only to feel safe, but to collaborate and cooperate. As Ibn Khaldoun puts it: 'Man needs to agglomerate in order to provide food and protect himself, and he needs to have a ruler in order to prevent people from invading each other's rights.'[2]

After the fulfilment of basic needs comes the organization of society. Rights must be protected by the rule of law, as human nature makes it inevitable that power and abundance will beget greed. Once we are protected from treachery, we need company, family and friends; we need to have neighbours, to see people walking by in the street, to exchange a friendly word or a smile. This cannot take place unless people are empowered to build a community on their own terms – and the communities designed by Galpin and Howard were created to 'feed the machine'. They were not centred around people as individuals, but around the Factory City checklist.

Ibn Khaldoun was describing a community built by people according to their needs: the food they prefer, the plants they use, the houses they appreciate, and so on. If we combine what nature provides and what people excel in, the result is usually a thriving community. In Galpin's and Howard's models, however, the provisions and needs were preset even before people arrived. The businesses of the Factory City or the Factory Village demand certain prototypes that the 'invited' residents must be deployed to create. But no matter how crowded it is, the Factory couldn't be a lonelier place.

Mass production leaves no room for the need to create, the need to make changes, or – most importantly – the need to own one's destiny. In 'organic' models, to be a farmer or to be a merchant I *choose* how to design my business model. The fact that I own my time, my effort and my product enables me to form connections and build relationships: I meet, I buy, I sell, I negotiate.

Although they were controversial and took place during turbulent times, the late 19th-century Ottoman reforms known as the Tanzimat represent an interesting attempt to acknowledge the social requirements that the Garden City model failed to consider. The Tanzimat marked a key moment in the recent history of the Ottoman Empire's regions. While there is still debate about the intentions behind the reforms, it cannot be denied that they have had a lasting effect on the relationship between people and land.

The Tanzimat came at a time when foreign powers were increasing their pressure on the faltering empire. The sinking Ottoman government was clinging to power, attempting to appease those who called for modernization of the old regime. Land reclamation was part of a general plan to rehabilitate the deserted lands of the empire. Chapter 3 has shown us how trade and agriculture were shoved into a tight corner – but in addition to that, a number of disasters afflicted towns throughout the Levant and Mesopotamia (Greater Syria and Iraq). The Black Death and earthquakes harvested lives at a point when the death toll from war and economic pressure was already high. Some cities in Syria reportedly saw their populations fall to a level below that of Roman times.[3] Consequently the land perished, labour became scarce, and people moved towards the west where rainfall was plentiful. Regions where rainfall dropped below 400mm a year were deemed not worth the effort, and were abandoned.[4]

Prior to the Tanzimat, land tenure had relied on Islamic law, which made a fundamental distinction between two main categories of land and the related rights of people. The first category was *miri* land: land owned by the state, which in turn grants the right to cultivate it (*tasaruf*, 'handling') to tenants – a right which is also heritable. The second was *mulk* land: land in absolute ownership. The owner has the right of *raqaba* (translated as 'neck', in reference to 'a hold of the neck'). This grants the freedom of cultivation as well as ownership.

Most of the agricultural land in the sultanate fell into the *miri* category, where grains were cultivated. The *mulk* constituted only a tiny proportion, concentrated mostly in orchards surrounding the villages.[5]

Over time, a third type of tenancy grew under the Ottomans. This concerned land that was cultivated in order to fund the military forces through the collection of tax revenue by military officers. In the 19th century, wealthy figures and government officials would bid for the right to collect this land tax – a certain proportion of which would be transferred to the government, while the rest would be kept by the collector. Further developments extended the grant from a leased period of time into a lifetime grant, which could be passed to heirs. These grants were called *malkhane*.[6]

The *malkhane* business empowered grant-holders independently from the state and allowed them to impose local rule for a short time, until the sultanate gathered up the reins for one last attempt at government before its fall. In its sitting duck position, the sultanate wanted to regain control and increase revenues from its vast lands in order to pay its increasing debts. By this time, however, the arable lands of the Fertile Crescent had been replaced by arid plains reaching to the boundaries of the Euphrates. Settlements were confined to the coastal areas, the mountains and the slopes on their eastern and western foothills.[7]

The historian Nuhad Samaan, whom I interviewed in Homs, shared with me some of his childhood memories concerning the creation of the villages, along with historical information about the Ottoman Land Reclamation Act in the Levant. Anyone who travelled across Syria today would see a completely different landscape from the one Samaan described to me.

Syria's recent rural landscape comprises a continuous stream of villages surrounding the cities to east and west. In this way, the cities are connected to each other by a network of fertility and familiarity. The villages begin in the south next to the Syria–Jordan border, where the cities of Daraa and As-Suwayda are flanked by fields of wheat and orchards of apples. They pass through Damascus, where the foothills of the Qalamoun mountains are home to cherry and apricot. The countryside continues towards the open fields of Homs and Hama, with their groves of olive and almonds, and cotton fields and peach orchards connect Hama to Idlib in the further north. Pistachio and olive tracts link Idlib to Aleppo to its east, where both are overlooked by the northern border villages on the foothills of the woody mountains beyond which Turkey lies. In its orientation from south to north, this central rural strip opens up to embrace each city to its east and west and reconnects travel routes to form a continuous living vein, providing supplies of goods and agriculture to the cities.

The coastal provinces are to the west of this central strip (on the eastern end of the Mediterranean); off the northern Lebanese border, this coastal strip is interrupted by the two main port cities of Tartous and Latakia. Trapped between the sea and the mountains, the villages dot the green foothills with citrus trees. Finally, a third strip shoots off from the banks of the river Euphrates and its tributaries in the north-eastern corner of the country, where grain crops surround the cities of Ar-Raqqa, Al-Hasaka, Dayr Al-Zawr and Qamishli.

Al-Badyia (the arid lands), the eastern parts of the provinces of Homs, stretching from the edge of the eastern villages to the Iraqi borders, along with Ar-Raqqa (southern parts) and Dayr Al-Zawr (south-eastern parts), make up the homeland of nomads and grazing lands, and an Ali Baba's cave of Syrian truffles. The three main strips merge, meet and branch around the country's rivers and their ancient urban settlements.

According to Samaan, this central rural vein connecting Homs to Hama to Aleppo is built on a geological fault line, to the east of which, for a long time, not much was happening. Until the 1810s, none of the villages you might see today on your road trip through Syria existed – and even the central ones around the cities were struggling to survive. The *mira* (grain tax) had dwindled significantly due to those harsh realities – and the importance of grain at that time can best be understood in comparison to today's fuel. 'Barley was the fuel of transportation, while wheat was the fuel of people,' Samaan explains.[8] The economy was paralysed by the shortage, and government reforms were required as a matter of urgency. One of the keystones of the land reclamation and agricultural reforms was the Ottoman Land Code of 1858. However, there were some reforms before this point: a ministry of agriculture was established in 1846 to stimulate production, and '[e]fforts were made to seden-tarize nomadic tribes, both to provide labourers for the cultivation of cotton and to subject them to taxation. Tax exemptions offered to villages for performing public services such as road building were abolished; new state agencies would perform these services.'[9]

This quote points to two important measures. First, the Ottoman government followed the example of ancient China, seeking to minimize the threat of nomads by settling them through agricul-ture. Second, the government sought to establish a direct relation-ship between citizen and state, replacing the social hierarchy that mediated between production and state. That is why the Land Code of 1858 was considered a benchmark, following which land tenure was altered all over the sultanate's provinces. The code made some changes to the categorization of land, adding three more classifica-tions to the *mulk* and *miri*. It was described as 'conservative' because it had retained much of the Islamic legislation; however, it was credited with two major innovations.

First was the 'obligation of landowners to register their land with the government and receive formal deed to the land'.[10] This allowed absentee ownership to take precedence over the previous right of occupation and cultivation, abolishing the authority of the tax collectors as mediators between landowners and/or farmers and the state. Now, ownership had to be registered and individual responsibility to pay tax could be determined.

Whereas this first measure was intended to increase revenue and re-establish state control, the second one was designed to reclaim land and encourage its cultivation. In principle, this second measure 'permitted individuals to own vast tracts of land as the state could issue deeds to formerly unoccupied land'.[11] So, except for the *mulk* and *waqf* lands (which were privately owned), the state had opened its lands to cultivators.

In Syria, the desertification of the eastern lands meant that vast tracts were left open to this second measure. People who deserted those areas for the higher rainfall to the west became, with the new law, more inclined to go back east to enjoy the rights of ownership. To minimize competition over western lands, the Ottoman government declared that the cultivation of eastern lands would exempt any felon or previously convicted individual from punishment for crimes against the state, such as avoiding tax or military service, debt, assaulting government officials and so on. The offer was a generous one: 5,000 dunum (500ha) would be granted to any person who showed commitment to cultivate the land over a period of five years, after which he could start paying for the land for another five years, after which it became his by right. Low prices were set for the lands, and the right was granted to extract from the land whatever it offered.[12] People could drill a well, excavate for building materials and so on – and building for residential purposes was also permitted. Furthermore, the code 'liberalized the right of bequeathing land, in the hope that keeping land within one family would lead to greater efforts to improve land'.[13] The lease from the state was only annulled where cultivation was interrupted for more than three consecutive years.

In this way, the whole series of villages east of the rain line crossing from Aleppo to Jerusalem was created virtually out of nothing. Around Homs alone, more than fifty villages sprang up over a period of roughly eighty years.[14] To this day, the villages bear the names of their builders: Nizariey (from Nizar), Murshed Samaan, Mukhtariey (Mukhtar), Husainiey (Husain) and so on.

Nonetheless, the law had loopholes of which some people were able to take advantage. City residents (particularly those with official connections) were first to hear of the changes, simply because of their proximity to the locations where the new measures were announced. Thus they were the first to act, before the city tradesmen and well before the villagers. Official inefficiency also allowed these people to register in places other than their own. They collected IDs from others, boosting their share from 5,000 dunum (500 ha) up to as much as 25,000 dunum (2,500 ha).[15]

Despite the intended reforms many individuals were able, by means of networking and administrative inefficiency, to hold unbelievably large tracts of land. One individual in Hisya (near Homs) reportedly acquired a share of 1 million dumun (100,000 ha) simply through official negligence, the surveyor having asked him where he would like the boundaries of his land to be. He pointed to two hills, and that was it![16]

In short, before the code, especially in the case of the vast *miri* lands, the state had leased land to peasants and granted them the inheritable *tasaruf* right to cultivate it. It also entrusted the job of land tax collection to powerful individuals. After the code, powerful individuals could own *miri* land and pay land tax directly to the state, and also lease the land to peasants to cultivate it in exchange for a quarter-share of the product. Thus the term *murabe'a* ('quarterer') was used to refer to the new kind of sharecropper peasant. The relationship between those powerful figures and the local peasants across different regions of the sultanate was dominated by fear and ignorance, exacerbated by a feeble government; and many powerful individuals benefited considerably from this social pathology. Countless peasants lost their property to moneylenders, many of whom, as described in the previous chapter, had businesses affiliated with foreign banks. In consequence, by the beginning of the 20th century 'large landholdings had been created and many peasants reduced to the status of tenant farmer or sharecropper'.[17]

The land-owning classes were not the only ones who benefited from legal loopholes. The law actually allowed property ownership to non-citizens, which offered the foreign powers great leverage, since they could operate from within the sovereign state. (This feature of the global economy has since become rampant everywhere, and is one factor behind the rise of nationalist movements worldwide.)

Nonetheless, despite the controversy around the Land Code of 1858 and the mistakes it made – some of which could have been easily avoided – we must give it credit for breathing life into Syria's dead countryside. Regardless of the law's intentions, it was designed with human nature in mind. The combination of exemption from small felonies, freedom to release the fertility of the land, channelling plans towards the most needful targets and granting inheritable rights, created real incentives for work and were a positive reinforcement of the rural economy. When family, future and fortitude are acknowledged, a person is not *alone* – a community is created.

On the other hand, the Tanzimat reforms, including the Land Code, should not be viewed independently of the context of their creation. The Young Turks (at the time still a secret society named the Young Ottomans) were pushing for further liberalization and Westernization; foreign powers were chipping away at the lands and institutions of the sultanate; corruption was rife among local rulers. All of these factors put pressure on the emerging society, and helped to shape what is now known as the Middle East.

Syria continued to slide into chaos. After the shift in the nature of property caused by the Tanzimat, the French occupation was on a mission to compartmentalize Syrian society on all levels, rural settlements not excepted. The goal was to establish a clear sense of private property. Forms of collective ownership had to be divided, divided plots of land belonging to a single landowner had to be agglomerated, and finally *miri* lands owned by the state had to be divided and rented to peasants. The aim was to establish a 'modern' system that would function in line with agrarian credit banks (which, again, did not conform with the Islamic legislation on which all these forms of land tenure were ultimately based). The vast swathes owned by powerful individuals continued to survive under the French mandate – some of them even expanded.

After the French, Syria's property became subject to socialist reclamation movements. The first Agrarian Reformation Code was issued in 1958 by a socialist government during the brief existence of the United Arab Republic of Egypt and Syria. It limited the ceiling of land holdings according to location, means of irrigation and amount of rainfall. Much smaller plots of land were permitted, and these became smaller still with subsequent acts (1963–70). During this time Syria saw the confiscation of vast tracts and change of their tenures under the motto 'Land belongs to those who work it'. By 1970, when the reforms were largely completed, more than 1.5 million hectares of land had been expropriated in this way.[18] One effect of these changes was an abrupt overturning of class structures and economic relationships.

The line of events beginning with the Ottoman Tanzimat and ending with the Ba'athist reforms show that there was no real feudalism in Syria of the kind attributed by Marx to the precapitalist society of Europe. Although large swathes of land were owned by a handful of individuals and 'notable' families, the customary laws and their local institutions (which are in essence fused with Islamic law) were predominantly – and to some extent continue to be – the means by which relations between landowner and peasant were conducted, the most important aspects being the 'quarter' share and the zero-interest loans. Moreover, the *miri* lands which were revived after 1858 as a life investment were in general held by people who cultivated them for generations. To accuse such people of 'feudalism' would be an injustice; the relation between landlord and peasant was more of a partnership. Many peasants relied on their wealthy partners to capitalize the agrarian process. True, the life of the peasant was no bed of roses and inevitably there were cases of injustice and exploitation – especially from the privileged francophone landowners. But feudalism as a class-based economic structure did not exist in Syria, and this was for two main reasons: Islamic law, which controlled shares and taxes (even when the state had a Westernized legislation), and the centuries-long existence of *miri* lands cultivated by people from all social classes, rather than by a single class of peasants. The socialists failed to understand any of this and began by attacking the colonizers, creating great chaos and complications.

In the aftermath of the current Syrian crisis, many analysts world-wide have been attracted by the theory that the conflict of 2011 was caused by a severe drought. The four years of drought between 2006 and 2011 were said to have been 'the worst ever recorded in the country'. According to the US Center for Climate and Security, the drought 'caused at least 800,000 farmers to lose their entire livelihood, and about 200,000 to abandon their lands'.[19] But this alleged correlation between rural migration to the cities and the drought has no basis – primarily because agriculture in Syria is a well-established ancient craft that depends on a comprehensive network of irrigation canals dating from before the Romans. In the absence of rain, people rely on reserves of groundwater that can be accessed through wells. This could explain why food prices remained relatively within their usual margins and the normal flow of crops into the local markets was maintained during the drought years.

In fact, the period 2006–11 saw crucial decisions that put Syria on the road to both agricultural decline and civic unrest. First, a five-year plan for an incremental increase in fuel prices was announced in 2006, sharply increasing the price of diesel. Agriculture was the sector most affected by this increase. Lured by the world's high market price for wheat, Syria had sold its strategic reserves of wheat in 2006, which meant that in 2008 the country had to import wheat for the first time.

On a more dangerous front, the law of property kept on changing with the rent laws attached to the unfolding story since the Tanzimat. In 2001, Law No. 6 was issued – called 'the new rent law' (as opposed to the 'old rent law' of 1970). The expropriation of land in the 1970s and redistribution of shares to the peasants was supposed to have meant that more peasants would cultivate the land. In fact, the reverse was true. Peasants had left the land to work in the newly opened factories in the city. This was not just because of the opulent promise of the city; it was because they couldn't carry the burden of cultivation alone. In the city, houses were rented to new arrivals in the old core, while the city began to sprawl towards the fashionable and newly built modern sectors – or even further, towards the hot shores of the newly discovered Petrol Gulf states and the European business affiliates.

The main flaw of the old rent law was that it had permitted no way for an owner to end a rent lease and claim vacant possession, nor any means to raise rent in line with changing market prices even decades later. The whole city was locked. Hence the new rent law, only thirty years late, was brought in to solve the vexed problem of 'old rents' – and its proposition was that the *owner* should offer the tenant 40 percent of the property's price in order to move out! Stories of blackmail, squatting, bribery, forgery and social crimes abounded. More migration from rural to urban areas followed, as did more emigration. In 2006, an amendment was passed to Law No. 6; it added the category of commercial shops and crafts to the properties subject to the new rent law. The whole city was effectively monopolized.

Both the 2001 law and the 2006 amendment had an execution period of three years, which meant the real turbulence occurred between 2004 and 2009. Meanwhile, back in the country, Law No. 56 of 2004 put the owner of arable land in the same position as the owner of city property, granting tenants the right to demand between 20 and 40 percent of the land in return for evacuating the rest of it (or, according to the tenant's wish, an equivalent payment in compensation). Again, given an execution period of three years, it was not until 2007 that this law wreaked its real havoc.

Soap operas were a popular mirror of this Syrian saga. In 2006, a hit TV series called *The Waiting* nailed Syrian viewers to their couches with its heartbreaking narrative of misery-drenched life in the 'informalities', or informal settlements. These were places on the city's edge, built without formal procedures and permissions, in which newcomers tried to make their home. *The Waiting*'s principal protagonist was an orphan who, Robin Hood-like, robbed from the stores selling mobile phones in order to share the profits with his needy neighbours. These neighbours shared complicated stories, all of which boiled down to the daily strife, loss of morality and blocked horizons of the concrete jungle.

A plot line that stood out was that of Samira, a mother of two boys and an employee, married to Wael, who is an employee too. Samira leaves Wael and asks him for a divorce, decades after having defied her parents in order to marry him. Her family is from the city, where her husband couldn't afford a house, so he has made a home for his wife and their children in the informalities. Samira has never been happy living there; but the breaking point comes when her son loses his sight in a street football match that ends with him and the ball under the wheels of a vehicle.

The title of *The Waiting* reflects its depiction of people trapped in an unhappy situation. To quote its opening lines: 'I'm waiting. I don't know what I'm waiting for. I'm waiting to live; I'm waiting to die.' A dozen similar series followed and in 2009, another masterpiece displayed the dilemma of Syrian social breakdown on national TV. *The Age of Shame* placed the individual struggles of a group of neighbours under the spotlight. Here too the writer followed the characters at work and in their flats, showing through monologues and dialogues that all of their dreams were broken on the shores of one rock: the house. This time, however, the setting was not the derelict informalities but the prosperous centre of the city.

Most of *The Age of Shame* takes place in the house of Abu Mounzer, elderly father of four adults who still live in the same house together with their bedridden mother. As a result of new changes in the law, Abu Mounzer's house is now worth 8 million SYP (the equivalent at the time of 160,000 dollars), so he takes two important decisions that will turn the life of the family upside down. The first is to sell the house so as to buy three apartments in the development projects outside the city for his children and himself; the second is to remarry, because his wife has been sick in bed for twenty years. The story sheds a special light on the female protagonist, Buthainah, who has sacrificed her life for the service of the family and served as principal carer for her sick mother. Throughout the story, the moral failures and darker aspects of each character are revealed. The threads of all their lives cross in the story of Buthainah, who secretly marries her friend's husband, gets pregnant, has an abortion, runs away, falls in love, and comes back again. In one epic scene, all the 'sinners' gather to cast their 'stones' on Buthainah, who in the end emerges as the only character who is morally admirable, making a selfless choice between her love and her duty to family. The writer's intention is clear in the title of the programme: by the end, it is as though he is saying to Syrian society as a whole, *Shame on you*.

For me, the real protagonist in this series was the property: Abu Mounzer's eight-million-pound flat. At the centre of all the crimes the characters commit – killing, bribery, deception, lying – lies the flat. The auctioning of it is an auction of neighbourliness, of family and of morals, with one objective: gain. The minute their home becomes an investment, to be folded under the armpit like a portable tent, the characters become more inclined to surrender to their darker sides, to reject each other and move in their separate spheres, no strings attached.

Like the Tanzimat, the dominating spirit of the decisions that led Syrian society into the age of shame was the so-called 'liberalization' of the Syrian market. The Syrian Factory City was marching at a steady pace towards the open horizons of the global economy, opening doors for foreign investors to step into the fertile lands of this old crescent and delve their hands into its soil for a fistful of ash that could be turned into gold. Except that the reverse happened: a country on fire.

To use Ibn Khaldoun's terms, in modernized Syria people have not been prevented from invading each other's rights; they have lost the means of collaboration to provide food; they have lost any real sense of shelter. In other words, we've lost the cornerstones of human settlement. On our way to losing home, we have been left on our own, in a jungle of the lonely.

Strict measures are needed in order to reverse the consquences of real-estate speculation that has allowed people to trample one another's rights. Before the war, it had become a trend in Syria for those who could afford it to buy multiple properties and hold onto them until the value increased, before selling for a profit. Property values shot up until few without an inheritance – or the profits from a diamond heist – could afford to buy. Of course, climbing the ladder in real estate has beome a modern business globally, not only in Syria; but we have no legislation to prevent it from being abused. We need to enforce a meaningful tax on multiple owner-ship, and take action to prevent communities being hollowed out by non-resident ownership.

Today, when reconstruction talks start over the devastated Middle East, we encounter plans like those in Egypt and Iraq, both of which simultaneously took the decision to ban the cultivation of rice (and in Iraq's case corn also) because those crops require 'too much irrigation' and there is insufficient rain. Is this a deliberate attempt to repeat our history of defeat – a sacrifice of local grain on the altar of the international Factory economy? Or is it a fit of amnesia, a failure to remember that in their flight from the land, people drag the tails of desertification behind them? The equation is simple: the less the land is cultivated, the less rain it attracts – not the other way around. Bad seasons and seasonal droughts have always been challenges to agriculture, in the face of which Galpin's men of the soil had to stand firm. The world's food security depends on the perseverance of those brave farmers, and – as the story of the Tanzimat tells us – the world's social security too depends on their existence. But this is not what the current governments of Egypt and Iraq apparently wish to believe.

In *The Introduction*, Ibn Khaldoun divides the northern part of the globe into seven regions. Settlement is most concentrated

Damascus, a Factory City on the march.

across the third, fourth, and fifth of these, owing to their mild climate and welcoming conditions. The mildest one is the fourth region. According to Ibn Khaldoun, the prosperity of these regions and the mildness of nature are reflected in the general behaviour and nature of the people, who thereby form 'the most moderate, and most temperate of societies'.[20] He points out that the second and the sixth regions are further from this state of mildness, and the first and the seventh are the furthest.

This correlation of the arability of regions with civilization is of utmost importance, as it draws our attention to the impact of vocations and businesses on people's minds and how all of this lies on the road from nature to exchange. It also clears away the clouded Western reports of the 'deserts of the Middle East', where the dunes of Dubai offer the only vivid mental image in the minds of their audience. The Fertile Crescent of the Levant and Mesopotamia is not a tale from the Thousand and One Nights. These lands, according to Ibn Khaldoun's map, belong to the fourth region, where the best conditions for agriculture exist and consequently the mildest of people. It is no coincidence that human civilization first thrived in this region, nor that today's 185,000km^2 of Syria (prior to the current conflict) turned into a country only a quarter of which is arable land.

The inner circle of supply around Damascus in the old days was not simply Garden City green belt. The orchards of Ghouta were an ancient paradise and a city's haven, where families gathered on the banks of water canals. The Ghouta is divided into Eastern Ghouta and Western Ghouta, both irrigated through a network of ancient canals and water mills connected by six branches dug from the river Barada. These works turned the Ghouta into a lush land of 370km^2 that produced an extensive array of crops and an interwoven economy of crafts and products. Along with the array of fruits, vegetables, grains, dairy products and the business of preserving, drying and processing, olive oil was used to make soap, and roses to make perfumes and rosewater. The furniture industry also relied on the Ghouta's wools, cotton, silk and walnut wood. But the historical processes recounted in this chapter and the previous one wrapped their poisonous threads around the Ghouta and squeezed the life out of it, turning 70 percent of its area into a graveyard of private factories and residential development projects. The Barada, like most of the region's rivers, turned into a stream of rubbish and waste water.

Before they surrendered to big business, Syrian cities traditionally had their neighbourhoods structured around what were regarded as forty primary occupations. This strategy of 'forty' didn't only build an economic system based on local production of essential supplies; it also created a social structure based on family businesses and a hierarchy of apprenticeship. Sheikh Al-Kar – 'Master of the Vocation' – is a social title unofficially granted to those who mastered an occupation over succeeding generations, developing the skill and ability to understand the inner workings of its world. Thus, local arbitrations within each vocation are settled by Sheikh Al-Kar. This was the means by which all Syrian crafts naturally preserved their refinement and evolution until the historical shift towards Westernization, and it also created a resilient social fabric.

In contrast to that, one of the strangest sights the modern city offers you is its pavement bookstalls. In Damascus, their 'headquarters' are located under the Victoria Bridge. Queen Victoria was supposed to visit Damascus in 1901, so a European-style hotel was built to accommodate her, together with a wooden bridge to cross the river Barada – but the Queen died before she could make use of either structure. Later on, the French military replaced the wooden with a metal structure, and eventually in 1968 the metal was replaced by poured concrete in order to carry the automobile traffic of the capital. But books were the addition which the property war added to this corner of the city. No literature can pay the rent of a city property; and between the profit from selling food or clothing and that from selling letters, illiteracy wins every time. The bookstalls mark one of the loneliest corners of the city; the whole history of cultural decline is expressed in those clothespegs fixing the books to wires above each stall. From the dignified tower of the Sheikh Al-Kar, our civilization has been dropped under Victoria's bridge.

Today, Damascus has been characterized by its governor and city officials as a 'services city'. This is what drives their vision for reconstruction – not the development of agriculture or small business, but a destination for tourists and a 'city of investment'. The

Book stalls under the Victoria Bridge in Damascus.

argument is pompously made with the same old buzzwords that have been in use since the Tanzimat: *modernized, civilized, internationalized.* The remaining islands of agricultural land that were gasping for air around the city have been submerged under the bloated towers and tasteless boxes of shopping centres.

Two main projects took place in the years of war in Damascus. The first was Marota City, announced in 2012 and intiated in 2017: a 214,0000m² development project that replaced the orchards of Razzi with dusty foundations, setting the ground for one of the ugliest structures ever built. The original owners of the confiscated properties were offered shares in the new business before they bid farewell to their lands and houses.

The second project was the gentrification of the ancient Hamrawi neighbourhood, which surrounds the Great Umayyad Mosque in old Damascus. The confiscation of this neighbourhood is an old story; it happened in 1960, after a great fire. Efforts to overrule the unjust and arbitrary decision have been made ever since. In 2016 Damascus sold the confiscated properties, which include a mix of houses and shops, to the investment company Damascus Holdings – the same company that is building Marota City. The Hamrawi project aims to turn old Damascus into a 'heritage village', where the centuries-old craft economy will become a puppet show of old caravanserai and an Eastern Mystic restaurant experience for tourists around the site of the Umayyad Mosque.

Buildings, like the people who occupy them, signal to us whether we can call them friends or not. Are we alone even in their company – or can we really *trust* them? The Great Umayyad Mosque at the heart of old Damascus is one of those buildings which has the power to embrace us, in spite of its colossal size. A walk around it shows the shops of the Hamrawi aligned to face the solid, 15-metre-high walls of the mosque. This kind of view usually calls forth a feeling of rejection, but the Umayyad seems somehow to induce quite the opposite. The historical layers exposed by the different sizes of stones in its walls spell out its journey, from the large pre-Roman chunks at the base piling up in gradation, to the smaller, clearer cuts of the Islamic Umayyad stone blocks; they gently invite the eye to look up towards one of the minarets punctuating the building's corners. These walls carry the imprints of the hands that the building has shaken, the gestures it has made and the bows it has offered.

The mosque's location has served the same function in different guises throughout the city's long history. First, the site was occupied by the Temple of Hadad, Aramaic deity of rain and thunder; then it was transformed into the Roman Temple of Jupiter. Later it was converted into the Church of St John the Baptist, and after that it became a jewel of Islamic architecture. Surrounding this spiritual locus, the busy markets of the city thrived over the centuries to become the pumping heart of the Silk Road. This central point between West and East represented a threshold between the materialistic and the spiritual, between reason and abstraction, which kept the world around it in balance and to which the city retreated every time it fell to its knees.

Architecturally, the Umayyad is distinguished by its lead-covered dome – the Eagle's Dome. But the mosque has witnessed so many tragedies and natural disasters (including seven major earthquakes) that it seems more of a phoenix than an eagle. The dome and minarets have collapsed, cracked and burned, but were quickly repaired. So too were its walls, gates and courtyard surfaces. In 1401 the mosque, along with the rest of the city, was burned by the Mongol leader Tamerlane; but that was only one of many fires it has survived. On each occasion, the mosque was saved by the Damascenes who lived in its shadow and cultivated life around it. Although various rulers initiated campaigns to restore the building to its glory, each reconstruction ultimately relied on *waqf* donations and the voluntary efforts of the people.

In a departure from that tradition of public spirit, a controversial restoration of the mosque was undertaken in 1994. The dismantling of the inner colonnade showed the true mettle (or metal) of the building: between each stone column and its base was a fine layer of poured lead that acted like a cartilaginous disk, creating a flexible 'spine' within the otherwise rigid structure. This hidden innovation had helped the building to sustain all those earthquakes and shocks, lasting in all its glory for twelve centuries.

Even the French clearances around the mosque failed to neutralize its approachability. Regardless of their beliefs, people wandering around the site are still tempted to place a hand or lay their head against the Umayyad's walls, so as to feel a little bit less alone in the changing city. I am no exception to this.

I stand barefoot at the mosque's western gate, having passed through the dark tunnel of the bustling covered souk. The freshly mopped floor of the courtyard feels so holy that I place my steps lightly as I cross towards the prayer hall. Flocks of doves are hovering overhead, mirrored by little children running around on the ground. As I move through the space, I pass individuals who have dedicated their lives to the service of the mosque; for a moment, the movement of people blurs with the background of the columns that have played an equally important part in keeping the building up.

Inside the prayer hall, I find a spot to pray while the stream of people, studying, visiting, worshipping, moves in continuous flux. I finish and head back to where I entered, seeing through the door the remnants of the Temple of Jupiter framing the opening to the souk, marking the crossing from one world to another. I leave feeling more connected, more in company with those around me, than when I arrived.

The souk around the Umayyad, however, is no longer the hub of communal collaboration and ethical trade that it once was. Changes in property law and the destruction of the social and urban fabric have eroded the meaningful qualities of the place. Still, one can find traces of that meaning in the exquisite mosaics covering parts of the walls in the Umayyad. As if speaking to us in coded messages, the

Damascus's fabric around the Great Umayyad Mosque, 1993.

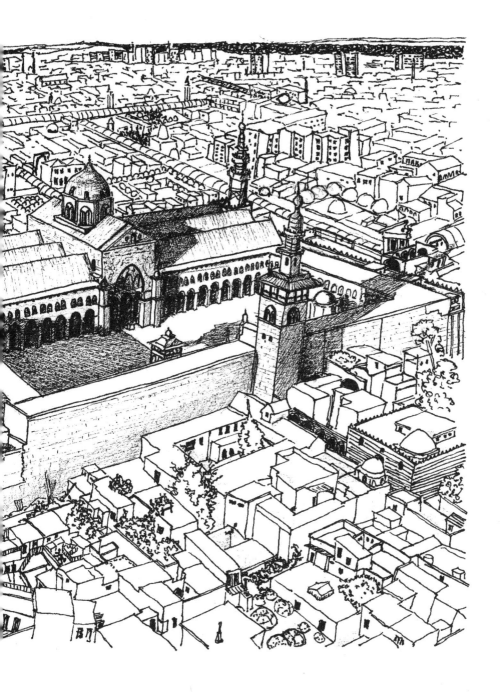

157

colourful scenes and intricate images of the main mosaic under the eagle's dome show a running river and tall fruit trees, with rows of buildings in between. Researchers disagree about whether these are representations of Heaven or a picturesque image of the river Barad and the Al-Ghouta orchards, two of the pillars on which life in this ancient capital once rested. The third pillar – the city centre, where God was worshipped and money was made – is collapsing under the pressure of the current service-oriented transformations.

For me, it doesn't get lonelier than this. We feel alone in the absence of meaning as much as in the absence of company. Therefore it is not only in empty streets that we feel alone; sometimes it is in crowded places like shopping malls, airports, train stations. We are most vulnerable when we suddenly find ourselves in a bubble of isolation. The background hum of those places where the blind rush of people is pretty much the only thing that happens was perhaps behind the attempts to introduce 'friendlier' designs for shopping centres; the enclosed box model gave way to one that allowed a more natural flow of movement, following the example of bazaars and souks.

In the English city of Oxford, the Westgate shopping centre is a project that stirred some controversy when it was first proposed. The building, originally designed by Douglas Murray in the early 1970s and comprehensively redeveloped in 2016–17 by Chapman Taylor Architects, has tried to fit into its surroundings by using earthy yellow limestone brick, bringing in natural daylight and ventilation through the open courtyard and including the spatial flow of a gateway. But it was criticized for the handling of excavations in the 1970s for its service basements, which destroyed medieval archaeological remains. Efforts were made to manage the redevelopment with more sensitivity, but it still destroyed additional medieval material for the sake of underground parking. The forbidding, windowless design of its south-west wall was also heavily criticized. Unlike the walls of the Umayyad, this new wall pays no respect to the remains of the past;

it feels imposing, rejecting, isolating. It signals loneliness. Outside the Westgate, small shops and businesses struggle. The new business in town is a global Factory with which they cannot compete, and which they cannot afford to join. This mega-magnet is voiding the old city and its shops of their customers.

Oxford, like Damascus, appears to have sacrificed its meaning to the business of tourism. If Oxford's small businesses had been better supported in maintaining a local craft economy, they might have had a chance to remain competitive. What shape could this support have taken? Neither city's own products are incorporated into its life cycle; nothing they produce is used directly for local building or other activities. For instance, if Damascus were to produce walnut wood – planted in the Ghouta, crafted in the city, manufactured for furniture and cabinetmaking, embellished by carving or inlaying – the immunity of small local shops would be much higher against the blight of a furniture factory. That's why big businesses do not typically enter such markets unless they can cut out the local trees or buy their orchards; and it is also in their

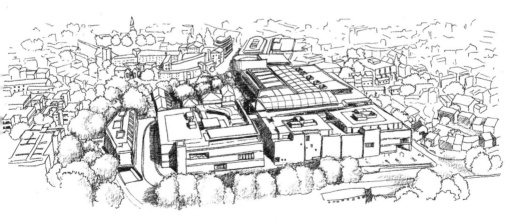

The Westgate shopping centre in Oxford.

interests to manipulate the public's perception of what constitutes a desirable interior, by labelling their own products as 'modern', 'smart' or even 'healthy'.

Oxford, of course, has the additional element of being a university city, colloquially expressed in the 'town vs gown' conflict – and then there is its colonial history. Both are important factors adding to its complexity, but the point I want to emphasize is that when big organizations like the Westgate occupy large swathes of property – usually in the hands of a single investor – they rely on the ability to attract swarms of people in order to cover costs and generate a profit. Part of their strategy is to raise the rent of their properties for retailers, who in turn must raise their own prices. For local businesses, this has a direct impact: raising prices in order to meet higher overheads is likely to cost them their customers. Or, if they are landowners, they will be tempted to rent out their property and move away to other locations. Tourism is the kind of activity that enables this cycle of spurious price inflation. The Syrian neighbourhoods of the forty occupations worked as an antidote to the influence of big business – and unlike tourism, local business and manufacturing provided local people with a counterweight to loneliness, a means of finding *acceptance*.

Jane Jacobs points to the inclusion of buildings of different ages as a means of diversifying a local economy. Neither Damascus nor Oxford is lacking in this regard. There is a powerful moral message in the presence of these buildings belonging to different eras. Like the presence of different generations of people in a single place, the buildings signal that this place accepts them. Like elderly people, ageing buildings are living proof of the continuity that has dignified them, of the generosity that has kept them living and of the willingness of their communities to protect them from harm. They show us that there is an alternative to the investment-obsessed, globalized economy, and in that sense they help us to ward off isolation and loneliness.

Balkrishna Doshi, the Indian architect and 2018 Pritzker Architecture Prize winner, has said that architecture should teach us how to 'connect with silence'.[21] Of course, the silence of loneliness is different from the silence of tranquillity – so how do we reach the right kind of silence around the cacophony of the Factory? The type of silence experienced in the Umayyad tells us that it is important for a building to achieve acceptance, to teach us by example, like a wise elder, how to fit in. Yet not all deals close successfully with a merging of interests. The main strand of social tension between city and village is the loss of acceptance, since each has been blighted by the other.

Agriculture is no easy craft and it imprints the personality with special qualities, as Galpin showed us. The Islamic *tasaruf* rights system that flourished in the Ottoman *miri* lands recognized this fact, creating an opportunity for people to work in a vast land that would justify the challenge. Vast lands mean large harvests – but they also mean high risk and great expense. In essence, the *tasaruf* said: expenses are on me (no credit) and work is on you. In a business requiring hard labour and life-consuming commitment, that might not seem like much of an incentive – but when the arrangement is inheritable, it becomes worthwhile.

However, it was this system of inheritable rights that caused the whole property business to crumble in Syria after the socialists' so-called reforms. At the first inheritance following the death of the generation of the confiscators, the smallholdings of tillage plots were effectively locked. I've mentioned earlier that after the expropriation and the 'war on feudalism', fewer peasants were inclined to cultivate the land. The land had become too small to be worth the effort, and the risk too high without the funding of an established partner. Hence the projected further division of land by inheritance had no horizon, and the peasants gave up.

The current generation of plot owners in Syria's villages are like the children of a father whose land produced a decent crop in the old days; after his death, they each have little chance of making a living from their single inherited share. Consequently, whatever remains in the villages is now being sold off for redevelopment into tourist-friendly projects: summer houses, motels, entertainment and recreation centres for the wealthy and for foreign visitors. In the same way, the old cores of the cities are eaten up by dead concrete blocks; the remains of the Syrian countryside, likewise.

Another issue to consider here is the education system, and how this conflicts with ruralism. Many studies of urbanization start from the assumption that everyone is already settled, middle-class and simply changing domicile. Set against that misconception, Ibn Khaldoun's observation that people are of existentially different kinds becomes both profound and urgent. If we can accept that different people want different things, it becomes apparent that our standarized education system is counterproductive.

If the young son of a farmer truly wishes to become a farmer himself, what drives him to spend many years in a system of mainstream education designed to set him on a different path? Based on what we've learnt in the previous chapters, the answer is simple: shame. Shame in the face of urban prejudice is what urges young future farmers to abandon their lands. The money that is gained by education is 'clean'; it has no soil on it.

If we wish to continue to eat food and breathe air, a system of education that supports rural life must become mainstream. The self-respect a farmer seeks in the modern world must be accessible in the form of rural schools and colleges teaching not only standardized lessons of grammar and mathematics, but the cultivation of the land and the humans who care for it.

Since the war closed Syria's airports, I have travelled across the border to Lebanon by car in order to take international flights. My taxi driver is a Christian ex-peasant who abandoned cultivation and the village to go to the prosperous city. Driving a taxi is what the city offered him, and it has become a fruitful business for him and his brothers. They run a mini-company of their own and all live in one block building they bought together – a small community of their own within the city. They still own land in their old village, but it has turned into a summer destination. All that grows there is the remains of what was planted a generation ago.

'Are you happy in the city?' I ask him.

He's not. 'Life is OK here,' he says, but the village is where his heart is. Why doesn't he go back? Obviously he can afford it. 'Well, because the land won't make me a decent living,' he explains. The land needs cultivation, and that means labour. In the old days, the whole family worked on the land. 'Women have changed!' he tells me. 'My wife won't work on the land like my mother did.' Couldn't he hire a farmhand to help? 'It wouldn't be worth it.'

The taxi driver's son loves the village, although he lives in the city. He takes every chance to go and sit up on the mountain with the cows, his father tells me. But the young man *has* to go to school – and he doesn't like that any more than he likes the city. How far he will succeed in suppressing who he really is, only time will tell.

Even if he has no home outside the village, the story of this driver and his family is more or less a success story; but it is surely not typical. In recent times, opportunities for rural migrants in the city have been extremely limited. For my driver friend, 'home' is the distant village and the city is merely a source of income. For his brothers, this has meant migration to Canada and Australia. Some sold their lands (especially those who received them due to the redistribution of confiscated property) so as to settle in the city; however, in the end the city rejected them just as they rejected it.

The process of property inheritance in the old city paralleled what happened in the countryside: a house that accommodated one family of six would become the shared property of six families of the next generation. But as we have seen, the city was deadlocked. Syria, like much of the world today, has become a Monopoly board for property investment rather than a *home* for anyone. Before the

Tanzimat, people were concerned with work, not ownership, and after the Tanzimat they became concerned with work as a means to acquire ownership – the beginning of the idea of property as an investment. The final blow came when socialist policies ensured that life was about neither work nor ownership.

Syria today has no farmhands to begin with, after all the losses of life and of land. But even if it had, 'it wouldn't be worth it', and in this it shares a destiny with the world.

The history of my country is, of course, a local one, but the dynamics of change are visible everywhere. Cities are becoming lonelier, and so are villages. In between, people are playing musical chairs. The wealthy and the retired head to dormitory suburbs while the less fortunate are pushed away from the cities they once lived in or tried to enter. Urban centres everywhere are becoming like Damascus, the 'city of services and investment' in which people are smudged into lonely areas with no social fabric and no history, while still trying to dress up and play their part.

Syria, the main stop on the old world's Silk Road, is today being incorporated into two modern undertakings: China's 'New Silk Road' and the Russian agricultural 'Green Corridor'.[22] Both are multi-billion-dollar projects with an intercontinental reach. China's strategy, with the slogan 'One belt, one road', is to create a global trade loop comprising one land road and one marine route, aspiring to take international trade to new levels of scale and speed. The Russian corridor focuses more on food and land products, with different treaties and different partners. Its relationship with Damascus, facilitating the mass export of Syrian agricultural products, was immediately reflected locally in higher food prices. In this global trade race, all the rich nations get involved: the US, the UK and Europe already have their own treaties and routes, crossing the world map with different projects and lines, but within the same competitive spirit as their global peers.

It remains to be seen what this will mean for those who live along these routes. But one thing is certain: agriculture and trade, the two crucial elements of the ancient world, are now being used to turn the whole of our modern world into a mass-production system of Factory Cities and Factory Villages. And this, as history tells us, always leads to famine and war.

5

THE FEAR OF BOREDOM
The Kaleidoscope of Meaning

In 2010, Damascus was ranked among the most expensive cities in the world for real estate. A capital from the 'developing world' had its place among the top ten! London was placed third, at 1,403 euros per square metre, after Hong Kong and Tokyo; Damascus was eighth, at 979 euros per square metre, after Moscow, Dubai, Bombay and Paris. Apparently, as a Syrian, I have a greater chance of buying a house in Singapore or New York – which came ninth and tenth – than in Damascus.

These results also compared the average salary of the Syrian citizen, then 300 US dollars a month, with the price of an apartment in a posh Damascene neighbourhood, then listed at five million dollars. What the report did not mention is that the price of one square metre in those residential neighbourhoods was estimated at between five thousand and ten thousand dollars, while in certain commercial areas the price could reach fifteen thousand dollars. Leaving aside the luxury areas, to buy a flat in Syria before the war meant that you needed at least 500,000 dollars in ready money in order to acquire an average apartment – which would probably cost you double by the time you were settled in and commuting to your place of work.

To get around this problem, Syrians built their own housing, illegally, in the 'informalities' I have previously mentioned. These informal settlements housed more than 40 percent of Syria's population before the war, and up to 60 percent in the aftermath. The main reason the government allows these areas – installing infrastructure and not executing demolition orders – is that the lands in question are primarily *miri* lands. Receiving this Islamic inheritance after the fall of the Ottomans, Syria's modern government found itself caught in a cleft stick: having to handle the legacy of family *awqaf*, *miri* land leases and shared ownership at the same time as it was busy scraping away the protective crust of Islamic legislation.

It's an open secret that countless properties in Syria are still legally owned by some Turkish families and in the name of the Sultan Abd Al-Hamid. There has been a chaotic mix of confiscation, illegal occupation of land by rural waves heading towards the city, and the conflicting series of rent laws described in the previous chapter. The government occasionally picks one area of the informalities to evacuate, so as to create a so-called 'development project'. Although it engages in social housing projects, most of what gets built is in fact used for market broking – a habit in which almost every Syrian who can afford it takes part. The property ladder has proved to be the fastest way up in a market whose every other indicator points downwards.

Today, after the war, the average Syrian citizen's salary is no longer 300 USD. For a time, while this book was being written, it dropped to about 30 USD as a result of the currency being devalued. Meanwhile, Damascus has made it onto a number of less desirable world rankings, such as the 'most dangerous' and 'most corrupt' cities in the world. Even so, its real estate market has more or less kept up with those of other countries. Below-average apartments are being sold for a hundred thousand dollars a unit, while rent prices have multiplied ten times in the regulated areas and seventeen times in the informalities.

Most of what was destroyed during the conflict was in the zone of the informal settlements. This has raised some eyebrows: could the destruction have been a kind of cynical demographic engineering? But anyone familiar with Syria's history understands that the violence erupted first in these areas not because economic pressures were more intense, but because the places themselves had grown from a mixture of injustice and social decay.

The informalities today are set to be rebuilt by property development companies. Syrian officials declare with pride that they will have high rises and shopping malls, so as to project the nation's 'civilized' face. Obviously their previous inhabitants will no longer be able to afford the rent; those who can prove that they once owned property there will be reimbursed in shares and become stakeholders. Do people mind? Some do, but the majority don't. If the property will prove to be worth the investment, most people are inclined to sell.

In order to prepare the ground for such an investment-prone environment ahead of reconstruction, a controversial new law was issued in 2018: Law No. 10. This law has occupied many pages of international humanitarian reporting and prompted much debate on the topic of 'demographic engineering'. It offered tenants three options: to become shareholders in the rebuilding, to sell their shares in public auction, or to establish their own contributing companies to invest and rebuild as part of the project. Considering that an off-plan, 100m^2 apartment in one of those recent projects in Damascus today is being sold for over 500,000 dollars, two numbers come to mind: the profit for the shareholders, and the number of those displaced.

For me, the most troubling aspect of this law is that it turns all people into investors, which kills any chance of fixing things. Everybody will be busy climbing the property ladder, which will inevitably lead to further crises. We have only to look at neighbouring Lebanon, a place from which most of the original inhabitants have had to flee – not because of immediate threat, but on account of an economic equation that doesn't add up. Some of them occasionally come back to visit the mother country, checking on their multiple *pieds-à-terre*, bought in hard currency for the sake of rent-out or investment. We in Syria are doing the same.

The usual tendency is to relate this situation to the war. To a point, this is reasonable; however, a quick look at cities around the world shows that the distinction between chaos in the colonized parts and order in the once-colonizing ones provides populations in both worlds with almost the same meagre share of space. Setting aside other differences, it becomes clear that the vast majority of people around the world are preoccupied with the dream of securing housing. The issue of housing provision has become a global concern and is a factor in many elections. That top ten list of the most expensive cities around the world for real estate says it all!

The regional planning models drafted by people like Galpin and Geddes were a roadmap for the industrialization of rural nature, in the same way that the Factory City required the industrialization of urban humanity. Like technology today, the automobile was a mass product, and is now produced and marketed on a scale far greater than is actually necessary. Indeed, contrary to conventional wisdom – according to which there is first the need, and then the thing that will provide for it – the age of industry has always operated in a reverse direction: 'Build it, and they will come.'

That motto was actually behind the building of Dubai. It was adopted by the nation for the construction of a prodigal dream that veneers the desert with concrete. Paraphrased from a line in the 1989 American film *Field of Dreams*, it succinctly explains how the age of the 'four revolutions' functions. Unlike the production of a cure for an illness, the infrastructure for cars, for example, preceded the need for their mass production. The American historian Eugene Rogan describes how, with the discovery of oil, the Middle East was transformed by the West from a society relying on animal power into a hydrocarbon society, surrendering the region to modernity and consumerism. Rogan shows how the American Council in Istanbul, both before and after the First World War, actively reported on the status of general roads in the Ottoman Empire – compiling statistics of American automobile sales in the region's markets, comparing them with the competing European provision and constantly watching for the moment when car fever might catch on.

According to Rogan, the widening of the roads came before the anticipated public desire for cars, prompted by the 'strategic needs' of war.[1] After the defeat of the Ottomans, the British and French actively continued the work of the late Ottomans in rupturing the fabric of the Islamic city. They flattened anything that stood in the way of their vehicles, while launching marketing campaigns that would encourage people to buy more of them.

Even uncolonized parts of the world were compelled by mass production to undergo this transformation. High-density urban populations require housing, which can be built in sprawls so long as the 'problem' will be fixed by transportation. Without its population, the land would need reclaiming – another 'problem' that could be fixed by company-led automation. This, happening in the wake of two major wars, means increased demand for housing and a lack of supply. A quick fix is provided by mass-produced new building materials that make fast construction possible; this in turn requires more cheap labour, more company-produced food, more transportation and more demand on housing. It almost makes you hear the drone of 'Everything is awesome!' – but even in *The Lego Movie*, characters wake up and realize the extent of the trouble ahead. So why do people keep joining the rush to invest in property? Why do they abandon their lands? What do they do in their share of space, within their share of time?

Being and Time (1927) is the German philosopher Martin Heidegger's famous dissertation on settlement, in which he discusses the concept of home in relation to those three crucial elements. In the previous chapters we have shed some light on the fears of need, loneliness and treachery. Those fears are experienced in relation to space, whereas the fear of death is linked to time. At the opposite end of the spectrum is the fear of permanence, in which a desire for change stems from an excess of stability: namely, boredom. While we enjoy the fulfilment of an established situation, continuity gradually loses its appeal and, in a panic, we seek meaning in the different and the new.

Another German philosopher, Arthur Schopenhauer, regarded boredom as one of the twin poles of human life, with the other being need, want, lack, or desire. He suggested that our urge to satisfy a feeling of lack or need drives us to pursue our desire; if we are fortunate, we capture it. But the satisfaction always falls short and we eventually feel boredom again, so we repeat the same cycle over and over. Schopenhauer defined boredom as 'tame longing without any particular object' and 'the sensation of the worthlessness of existence.'[2] This state of metaphysical emptiness has been considered by many other philosophers, from Seneca to Blaise Pascal and Søren Kierkegaard. The consensus among these thinkers is that boredom is a default state of the human condition from which we constantly, desperately try to be diverted.

But not all boredom is as dramatic as that suggests – sometimes, one can simply be frustrated by one's limited ability to pass the time in a waiting room. And no one was able to delineate the difference between various modes of boredom better than Heidegger.

In *The Fundamental Concepts of Metaphysics*, a collection of lectures published in 1929–30, he suggested three varieties of boredom: 'becoming bored by something', 'being bored with something' and 'profound boredom'. The academic Jan Slaby, in an excellent paper from which I will borrow in what follows, explains the subtle differences among the three.[3]

The first variety of boredom, 'becoming bored by something', results from the inability of something or someone to lead us to an expected fulfilment.[4] Heidegger gives the example of a person waiting for a delayed train at a village station, 'killing time' until it arrives. The postponed fulfilment here is the arrival of the train and his need or desire to board it. Similarly, we might describe a book as boring if we don't find in it the sought-after thrill, excitement or wisdom.

In the second variety, 'being bored with something', we cannot determine precisely what it is that is boring. Heidegger describes attending a dinner party at the end of a working day: the gathering is exactly as expected, a pleasant experience where everything from food to company and conversation goes well – and yet it is boring. Our fear of boredom here is rooted in the fear of *wasting time*: Heidegger sees the dinner party as a missed chance to do something more meaningful.

This might sound melodramatic: surely not every single moment in life needs to have a meaningful impact. What does 'meaning' mean? Isn't it meaningful to meet people? When is it time to simply have some fun? What *does* matter? The answer leads us to the third variety of boredom: profound, all-encompassing, unconditioned boredom.[5] This type of boredom is 'an existential extreme....A non-person, a "no one" is facing an all-encompassing void. This, in turn, leads to a third dimension of emptiness: Non-self and insignificant world are related in a mode of "unrelatedness".'[6] In this deep state of boredom, passing time is no longer possible. Instead, we become ready to unlock a great moment: the *Augenblick*, or 'moment of vision'.[7]

Heidegger's optimism concerning this 'moment of vision' is founded in a correlation between an acknowledgment of the limitedness of time in human life and the freedom to use it consciously, 'freely and responsibly taking charge of our existence'.[8] What we can take from his analysis is that we are born with this concern to find answers to the existential questions: what really matters? What makes a difference? What is meaningful? We can't bear the thought that we have passed through life leaving no mark, that our existence and our non-existence would have been, for the world in which we live, one and the same. It is in our nature that we have to have a purpose, and it is in the nature of our universe that there is a time limit on finding out what that might be. Our fear of boredom is nothing more than a fear of failing at this task.

Turning all people into 'investors' is the ultimate distraction from Heidegger's *Augenblick*, for it takes people away from their effort to find meaning. We find meaning in our human contribution, in what we bring into the world and the impact this creates on others. The more people who benefit from our contribution, the more meaningful it becomes. How else can we 'freely and responsibly' take charge of our existence? That dinner party might not have been so boring for Heidegger if he hadn't been constantly thinking about better ways to use the 'lost' time.

In times of war and pandemic, we are faced with such existential questions: can we live like lab rats, confined and concerned about life's 'essentials'? What kind of impact can our virtual communication with people make? Enough that we no longer think of the time in confinement as 'lost'? For how long can we maintain such a life?

During these times we also question our means of making a living. Curfews, quarantine and besiegement expose the fragility of not only our lives, but our business models. All of us depend for our survival on land, without which we end up fighting over boxes on supermarket shelves. It is the land, not the Factory, that keeps us wearing our humanity. But when land is sacrificed to business – as we've seen in the example of the old Levant – we have a real problem.

Property investment is an unproductive means of making a living, contributing little to the common good. Although it may be an extremely lucrative source of income, it is a sterile form of trade: being so abstract, like the trade in money, it does not transform itself into other forms of production. To use the analogy of the ecosystem again, this kind of 'trade' is *indigestible*; therefore, it cannot belong to the ecosystem. Instead it forms its own cycle, producing abstract growth that translates into numbers instead of lived subsystems. That's why it is sterile, and why it ultimately has only a negative impact in the form of increased house prices, increased homelessness, social problems, health problems and the rest.

Damascus represents an interesting example of these two cycles running against each other, resulting in war, and yet still continuing. Before becoming one of the least affordable cities in the world, it had always offered a home to the homeless. As a Homsi, I've always been fascinated with Damascus's particular charm. In our adolescence my friends would come back from short trips to the capital with a strange gleam in their eyes, brought about by spending time in the city where everything seemed to be available. Those who studied at Damascus University would assume an instant academic superiority which was only reinforced if they managed to find work in the city. Weirdly, most of those who come to live in Damascus, even for the shortest amounts of time, return to their towns and villages with an affected Damascene accent – one that stretches the end vowels of words and, in more extreme cases, delivers speech with a slow and constant nasal intonation.

Those enchanted in this way speak of the rich cultural life and sophistication of the capital, and how Damascus is 'at least a century ahead of us'. It gets really annoying at times, when the endless comparisons depart from logic and turn into infatuated statements like 'Well, Damascus is just nicer,' or 'The Damascenes are different from us; they just know better.' Why does one city, struggling with the same challenges as others in the same country and the same 'problematic' region, seem to enjoy such elevated status?

For many, the appeal of Damascus is its sophistication. Like all capital cities, it has traditionally hosted embassies and diplomatic missions; it has been a centre of cultural exchange and high-profile events. In support of such activity, Damascus distinguished itself from other Syrian cities through a landmark building: the Assad Library. This, the only public library of its kind in the country, was built in the postmodern style, overlooking the Umayyad square from a sloped triangular piece of land to the west.

As a result of a collaboration between Syria's Ministry of Culture, UNESCO and the International Union of Architects in Paris, a design competition for the library was announced in 1973. Among its eight members the assembled international jury included French architect Michel Ecochard (notorious as the architect of the French mandate in Syria) and Aleksander Franta, president of the Polish architects' syndicate. In 1974, the winners were announced. First prize went to the Polish architect Jan Jacek Meissner; second prize was won by a Syrian architect, and third shared between Syrian and Bulgarian architects. The Polish win was in line with a trend during this period for the export of Polish architecture and urban planning to the Middle East, resulting from collaborations between Poland's government and its counterparts in a number of other nations. Along with Meissner, three other Polish architects are credited as the design team for the national library in Damascus: Małgorzata Mazurkiewicz, Marek Dunikowski and Wojciech Miecznikowski.

The library takes the shape of an oblong monolith, 100m long, 33m deep and nine storeys high, with a mezzanine and two levels of basement. By making the plan L-shaped the architects added an adjoining four-level rectangular annex to the left front of the building, which houses facilities accessible from both inside and outside the library: a café and terrace with a theatre underneath. Above the terrace is an enclosed reading room.

The library's six levels are served with six lifts and three service stairs at the rear edge of the rectangular plan. The internal space is divided into two atriums, each serviced by a spiral case surmounted with a cupola below the flat roof of the marble-clad block. From the outside, the building looks sober, with elegant vertical panels of light pink and beige marble intersected by horizontal bands of opaque glass windows, one of which is curtained with corrugated metal panels.

The interior cupolas and the *ablaq*, together with the pink strips on the exterior, might have been the architect's response to the Syrian request for a building that keeps 'within the characteristics of Arabic architecture while still adapting to a modern image'.[9] Regardless of the concept, the building has a mysterious, impressive and elegant quality. Its upper floors (the fifth and the sixth along with the roof's level as the seventh) constitute a single windowless block, creating a sophisticated visual balance between openness and solidity, vertical and horizontal, black and white.

Rarely is such a solid space on a building's elevation possible, because all human activity requires ventilation and lighting. Windows are essential, unless a space is used only for storage. And that is exactly the function of the fifth and sixth floors of Al-Assad Library – a book stack. The weight of books is enormous, which is why libraries tend not to stack their collections above their buildings; however, in this case the bedrock of the building, which stands on the valley of the river Barada, posed a major challenge. Damascus is located in a river basin with large natural reservoirs of groundwater. It would have been impossible to build book stacks into the foundations while keeping them dry enough for the items to survive.

Construction of the library was handed over to the Institution of Military Housing. It began in October 1978 and was completed in November 1983; the library opened the following year. During the building phase, the project was taken in hand by Raghib Aswad, the private consulting architect of President Hafiz Al-Assad, with the consent of the designing architect.[10] Its total cost was officially reported as 102 million SYP. Ahead of the official opening, in January 1984, a British consultant called A. E. Jeffreys was sent to Syria for four weeks. His mission was 'to establish general guidelines of Al-Assad's National Library, in close cooperation with the Ministry of Culture'[11] as part of UNESCO's Special Account for increased aid to developing countries.

In his report for UNESCO, Jeffreys delivered a comprehensive assessment and recommendations for the development of the library. His remarks addressed the different requirements for establishing a successful modern library – and by modern, he meant Western. After visiting the building during the final stages of construction, Jeffreys' report comprised eighteen pages of

The Assad Library in Damascus, overlooking the Umayyad Square, with Mount Qasioun in the background.

technical notes on how to put the Al-Assad Library on the right path ahead of its upcoming inauguration: from aims and objectives, capacity and future prospects, building up the collections, designing the administrative structure, training the staff, indexing books and plugging into the international digital world, together with publicity and funding. The British Library was used a couple of times as a prime example and an international training course was advised for the teams of potential librarians, in connection with which Syria lacks all educational infrastructure. The report stressed the importance of having 'aims and objectives more clearly stated', continuing: 'It can't be all things to all men' – which reads as ironically funny to anyone who has done business in Syria.[12]

By the time of its opening, the library's purpose had become clear, as the website declares: 'to gather all books and daily issues in addition to all kinds of literature connected with our ancestral cultural legacy; then to sort out these materials to serve researchers and scholars and benefit them'.[13] This seems like a good, clear objective. The only problem is that the 'ancestral legacy' turned out to be the great bulk of the Islamic collection from the much older Al-Zahiriyya Library, formed mostly of *waqf* endowments. This means that the books making up the main collection of the Al-Assad Library are in fact endowed properties subject to the *waqf*'s conditions, rather than to the international ISBN and ISSN scheme called for in the Jeffreys report.

Before functioning as a library, Al-Zahiriyya, built in 1276, was a madrassa: a school of theology and other fields of knowledge. It was built by the Mamluk ruler Sa'id, fulfilling the will of his father, Zahir Baibars. It stands at the core of Damascus, north of the Umayyad Mosque, adjoined by an array of madrassas built in the periods of the Ayyubids and Mamluks. Like most such Mamluk and Ayyubid buildings, Al-Zahiriyya is also a mausoleum, where the bodies of the Zahir and his son Sa'id are buried.

With its elongated *muqarnas* entrance, pink-and-white *ablaq* façades and exquisite interior bands of mosaic, the building is not only a prime example of Mamluk architecture; it is also considered the oldest library in Syria. It became in the time of the Ottoman sultan Abd Al Hamid one of the most notable libraries in the whole of the Islamic world. Its collection was expanded in interesting times and in controversial fashion. In an agreement between the Ottoman ruler of Damascus, Medhat Pasha, and the political and religious notable Sheikh Taher Al Jaza'ari (Al Jaza'ari referring to his original country, Algeria), Sheikh Taher made it his mission in 1881 to gather the scattered *waqf* collections of books from the numerous madrassas and *zawaya* ('corners', meaning small-scale teaching corners) in order to keep them in one safe place – Al-Zahiriyya. To that end, the madrassa was officially recognized as a public library under the chairmanship of Sheikh Taher.

Some reports say that the collection gathered from ten main *waqf* libraries exceeded 75,000 rare manuscripts and thick volumes. Interestingly, reports also refer to 'books being hidden from the gathering campaign' and 'vicious resistance to the efforts of Sheikh Taher, some of which reached the level of death threats'.[14] The main reason for that resistance was fear of the loss of books and mismanagement of *awqaf* endowments. I couldn't find any reference explaining the source of those suspicions of Sheikh Taher, but perhaps those who feared for the collection had some prophetic hunch that it wouldn't remain in Al-Zahiriyya after all.

Deprived of its main collection, the building underwent two major restorations: one in the 1960s, which used cinder blocks and cement and distorted the building almost beyond recognition, and the other executed more skilfully between 2007 and 2011, funded by Kazakhstan. Apparently, Kazakhstan's president visited Al-Zahiriyya in 2007 and was not very impressed by what had become of the legacy of his hero ancestor. So he offered the Syrian government a generous restoration fund, amounting by the end of the project's first phase

The main courtyard of Al-Zahiriyya Library.

to 100 million SYP – almost equal to the total cost of building the Al-Assad Library. The second phase, which was interrupted by war, aimed to expropriate the surrounding properties (many of which are themselves *waqf* foundations) in order to create a 'cultural axis' for the dream vision of a touristic old Damascus.

The story of these two libraries, Al-Assad and Al-Zahiriyya, trying to fill their shelves with meaning that constantly eludes them, encapsulates the history of all the shifts in that meaning – not only in a capital like Damascus and in a country like Syria, but also in a wider region that is shredded between two worlds, torn by colonial complexes and burdened by an undefined legacy.

As architecture students, my friends and I used to tune in to the Damascus Book Fair, at which international publishers would exhibit their new releases. This was a rare sight compared to the sheltered life we led in our home towns. The university campus in Damascus had libraries filled with new releases and sourcebooks, while the bookshelves in our colleges – whether in Homs, Hama, Tartous or other Syrian cities – comprised the slimmest of collections, containing only students' research notebooks and perhaps a personal selection made by some professor in the course of a recent visit to Damascus.

Damascus was not only a seat of power and authority. It was also the 'good' face of Syria, constantly being polished for the eyes of the world to see. The rest of us, out of sight, hardly mattered. Furthermore, most Syrian government institutions are centralized in Damascus – overloading the capital with a floating population of millions of people who leave her at night and flood back into her in the day. In such circumstances, the city's businesses thrive disproportionally to the rest of the country, and its standard and cost of living are matched only by those in Aleppo. Money definitely resides in Damascus; but there are many nuances to this fact.

Just as there are two libraries, there are two Damascuses and indeed two Syrias, the differences between them sharpened by eight years of war. One Damascus holds the seeds of life, the other the sickles of death. The first is the Damascus of Fairness, where trade takes place; the second is the Damascus of Vanity, where leisure and money laundering dominate. These aspects of the city's nature are intertwined in its physical structure, but distinct in character. Old is mixed with new, rich with poor, conservative with liberal – but one face of the city is work-driven while the other is leisure-driven.

Damascus has exhibited a kind of duality throughout its history, taking the forms of both a Greco-Roman and an Aramaic-Oriental city. The 20th-century historian Jean Sauvaget described it as *une ville double*, although it ultimately developed along its original Oriental model.[15] This made the city unique during the Roman era, having two parallel columned streets instead of the usual one. Even its temple, which eventually evolved into the Umayyad, had double courtyards.

Today, its duality remains unreconciled. In what I call Fair Damascus, the city is a bustling throng of business, taking up the ground floors of whole neighbourhoods radiating out from the old Al-Hamideya Souk. Businesses exist in highly specialized clusters: if you are searching for light equipment or electrical tools, you head to Al-Marjeh Square. Books and stationery are found in Al-Bahsah and Al-Halbouni, furniture and high-end household goods in Al-Abed street, clothing in Al-Hamrah and Al-Salhiye, and so on. There are markets for paints, car repairs, dentistry equipment, textiles, food.

Damascus shows its ability to service an intricate web of needs, providing an infrastructure of goods that is rarely seen compressed and distributed in such an individualized way anywhere else in the world. And the way the market is laid out is an important element of the city's charm and sophistication. Its individual traders, who mostly belong to long-established family businesses, are highly experienced in assessing each shopper, capable of pushing exactly the right buttons to make a hesitant customer take the leap into their warm world of deal-making. This shopping experience is nothing like that of a tourist trap, where quality is uncertain and the real price hides under a raised tag, waiting to be fished out by bargaining. In fact, the Damascene trader dislikes bargaining and shows impatience towards customers who insist on it. He prefers a more straightforward way of doing business. The price is already exposed through the cluster of competitors a few feet away in every direction. 'See my neighbour' is a commonly heard phrase at the various shops. The souk's traditions are kept alive in the network of modern markets all over Fair Damascus.

This Damascus is widespread and cannot be covered on foot – and here arises the problem of traffic, an unpleasant aspect of all modern cities in this region owing to random and improvised planning. But for the controversial ring roads which have cut the city from its green belt and created hard boundaries between it and the surrounding suburbs of the Ghouta, the congestion in Damascus would be as bad as in Beirut. As it is, there is room for a decent flow of vehicle movement despite the lack of public transport. Nevertheless, parking remains problematic despite the presence of multi-level parking venues near the city's hotspots. Streets are constantly clogged with cars jostling for spaces. Near every cluster of markets there are usually one or two public institutions; this means an additional flood of employees, security staff and visitors all cramming the commercial space.

In this flux, all features of the urban place – street, pavement, buildings, shop windows – seem fused together by the crowds. The scene is dotted with the white hats of policemen, rising like sharks' fins above the waves of people. They stand in their black uniforms with a relaxed posture, holding their open ticket books with a pen resting on the paper, ready for the prey to fall into the trap. It could be a desperate attempt to park in a lot left for an important official, or it could be a forgotten seatbelt or a mobile phone.

In this respect, Homs might as well be on another planet. Here, people feel that they do you a favour by stopping at a red light, and seem shocked if a policeman tries to enforce any law. Businesses too are quite different from those in Damascus. There are no such crowds, variety, competition or marketing. After losing its means of local production, the only cluster of specialty Homs was left with was the food vendors, and this is reflected in the morals by which business is conducted. The typical Homsi trader is much less patient than the *Dimashqi* (Damascene) and shows little will to make any effort towards the customer. Business is done with a 'take it or leave it' approach and a higher price tag than can be found in Damascus.

The face with which Fair Damascus greets you makes it clear why Homs is characterized as a 'village' in comparison to the great city. Trade is the essence of a city; however, Fair Damascus shows us that it is not just *any* trade. It is the trade that manages to form a code of conduct in relation to its urban capacity. It is the trade that can be 'digested' in the ecosystem of the city. This trade, guarded by the remnants of *waqf* buildings and family legacies, is slowly disappearing as a different way of life marches towards it under the banner of 'reconstruction'. This newer way of life is embodied in what I think of as Vanity Damascus: modern towers overriding ancient architectural jewels, old houses turned into genteel restaurants, multi-million-dollar apartments opening as beauty centres. All of these are owned by the same handful of people, but they are gradually creeping forward to take over the city.

I visited Damascus recently with my family. Looking at my son, I found him making a weird expression, half-opening his eyes, turning his upper lip downwards and slightly opening his nostrils so as to appear somewhere between disgusted and depressed. Then he said: 'Why do people here look like *this*?!' And he made the face again. 'People in Homs don't look like that.' It was an accurate observation, as Homsi features do tend to appear more relaxed; this was the case even during the city's darkest days. Perhaps it is something to do with the fact that they don't feel as threatened by vanity as the Damascenes.

Vanity Damascus is not only an expression of emptiness and loss of meaning – it is a manifestation of inequality. People who try to express these concerns are often misunderstood as simply advocating for heritage, which in turn can be another form of 'vanity'. But in fact their objections are genuine calls to action that require reactivating the role of those older buildings, not as empty shells for nostalgic performances, but as living organs in an ecologically integrated settlement.

In his 1979 book *The Timeless Way of Building*, Christopher Alexander warns of the loss of 'the natural processes of building towns' in favour of less satisfactory replacements, for which he largely blames planners and architects:

> *Since the natural processes of building towns no longer work, in panic, people look for ways of 'controlling' the design of towns and buildings.*

Those architects and planners who have become concerned by the insignificance of their influence on the environment make three kinds of efforts to gain 'total' design of the environment:

They try to control larger pieces of the environment (this is called urban design).

They try to control more pieces of the environment (this is called mass production or system-building).

They try to control the environment more firmly by passing laws (this is called planning control).

But this makes things still worse.[16]

Alexander seems to have accepted that the 'natural processes' on a comprehensive scale have been defeated beyond return. He proposes a 'pattern language' – by which sequences emerge from a root design – derived from the natural processes, as a way of counteracting the toxicity of current ways of building. In his disapproval of the work of planners and architects, he asserts that the 'right' way of space creation was natural to people before it was forgotten by our modern ways. In a sense, he seems to be open-sourcing architecture as a profession to anyone who has a reasonably good eye. He also seems to place the blame for all the mistakes of modernity solely on the shoulders of architects.

He is not alone in this conclusion. Roger Scruton has said that:

The first principle of architecture is that most of us can do it. You can teach music, poetry, and painting. But what you learn will never suffice to make you into a composer, a poet, or a painter. There is that extra thing, which the romantics called 'genius', without which technique will never lead to real works of art. In the case of architecture not only is the part that can be taught sufficient in itself, but also the belief that you need something else – genius, originality, creativity, etc. – is the principal threat to real success.[17]

In my view, both Alexander and Scruton, if not mistaken in their criticism *per se*, are focused on the wrong tender spots. The first principle of architecture is not that most of us can do it – on the contrary, only a few of us can actually do it right. Some of us are lucky enough to live in homes we can claim as our private worlds, and because we are entitled to change things and move them around, we begin to feel we understand architecture. But this is no more true than to say you are a physician just because you can prescribe yourself a painkiller or bandage your own simple wounds.

That 'extra thing' Scruton refers to, and 'the quality without name' Alexander speaks of, are indeed the secret behind our admiration and appreciation of what we all agree to call 'great works'. The threat didn't stem from the ambition of architects to master their works – the whole history of architecture tells quite a different story. The real threat actually arose when architects signed up (willingly or not) to the cycle that runs against Alexander's 'natural processes'. This is the cycle created by the Factory's appropriation of building resources, which has reinvented building on an industrial model. This reinvention was made possible by the political decision to hand lands over to investors, offering an open invitation to people from all walks of life to hold a share in it.

In the older system, which both Alexander and Scruton value, people were part of a cycle that processed nature from two ends: the producer, who cultivates land, and the processor, who processes the land's products. This system was able to thrive by providing quality materials for building and employing an array of people who could engage in the crafts involved in production. The cycle provided a coherent system of building elements that relied in turn on a system of businesses, which then fed back into the cycle: being a carpenter, blacksmith or mason, I ensure a place for my craft in the overall scheme of things.

In this cycle, the architect is a space maker – exactly like a dressmaker. He or she uses teams of experts who provide the good fabric, the nice embroidery, the right stitches, and so on, but only the architect can make the best decision as to what goes where.

It takes a real expert (and despite its controversial meaning, I'm going to say *an artist*) to 'make a work of art by simply combining patterns', as Alexander notes.[18] For even if you have the patterns, it is no simple task to combine them. Unless architects are allowed access to the right type of cycle, they cannot produce meaningful creations. The great sin committed by modern architects – for which they deserve to be castigated by Alexander and Scruton – is that they have enabled and promoted the wrong cycle. But this is not a reason for condemning their art; only their abuse of it.

In the same article, Scruton expresses appreciation of the rows of buildings on Ankara's hilltops as a successful example of how dispensable architects can be: 'They join together to form charitable associations, so as to build mosques in the ancient style and neighbourhood schools beside them....And they are produced in just the way that sheds are produced, by people using their God-given ability to knock things together so as to put a roof over their head.'[19] But he should recognize that this is the result of the *waqf* idea, rather than a 'God-given ability'. *Waqf* is what drives people to build mosques and schools and endow them as God's property, inaccessible to the profit-making zeal of the investment culture. You only need to look at the informalities on the hilltops of Damascus or the *favelas* of São Paulo to realize how easily the result can take a different course.

Because the publication of my first book came at a time when the international media had its eyes fixed on Syria, people would ask me in interviews, 'How would you fix this?' and 'Where would you start?' My answers never seemed to satisfy them, because usually in such situations people look for brief, reassuring, simple answers – political statements, in short. Instead, my belief was that no one person would be able to propose a solution so as to say, 'Hey, here is a plan: just get it funded and all will be well.' Before the actual rebuilding, we need to rebuild the network that we've lost, and that is no easy task. It won't suffice to have a 'pact of sects' or a 'gender balance', as many of those who get involved in the region's issues would like to see. The 'one of each' approach seems to me a rather superficial one, showing little understanding of how human settlements can flourish, of 'umran – and putting the cart before the horse. Social justice is a result of a fair ecosystem, not of the policies of those who manage it. The Ottoman neighbour-hoods of the forty occupations, the system of the miri land, and the awqaf all prove this point.

Think of a simple building element, such as the window frame. Not too long ago, carpenters in Syria were responsible for providing these elements – not for a mass market but rather an individual, case-by-case market. The selection of the right characteristics for each individual frame, starting from the quality of wood down to the smallest detail in the final form, was part of a process that had its own tested expertise. It was part of a web of understanding of local people's tastes, local materials, other elements, other voca-tions and other buildings – a 'pattern language', as Alexander aptly calls it, a 'generative grammar' of vernacular building.

This created a network of people whose work was in every aspect interdependent: wood suppliers, carvers, painters, even chemists who formulated special coatings for the final product. The result was a generally sophisticated style and a sense of ownership and belonging; not only that, but it enabled a cycle of businesses and a network of collaborations reminiscent of the specialized trade clusters that bloom in Fair Damascus.

This system has been destroyed by a number of processes, many of which have already been explored in this book. The damage began with the building legislation and expropriations that con-fiscated properties or made them too expensive to be used for these vocations. This in turn raised the prices of the products, making them unaffordable. Tradesmen were too vulnerable to fight back

The informalities on the hilltops of Mount Qasioun in Damascus.

against the planners, and the city authorities wanted them out to make room for property investment. Trades were pushed out of the city into the industrial peripheries under different pretexts – whether the pressure of internal migration or the vision of a 'civilized city' that cannot tolerate the sight of human labour. The exiling of these artisans not only increased their costs and consequently their prices; it also cut their connections with ordinary customers. They were being pushed into Factory mode in order to survive.

Having created this void in the market, the final blow was the arrival of cheap materials imported to fill it: Chinese building elements (window frames, in our example) that promptly flooded the market. Mass-produced and instantly available on demand, they became the basic diet of the building industry. Like fast food, they had a bland taste, and caused an adrenalin rush and permanent health consequences. In place of the beautiful, durable wooden windows that had been in harmony with everything else around them and could be passed on from generation to generation, the new plywood is ready for replacement at the first hint of boredom.

It is worth remembering that before it became the world's largest factory, China – after whose most famous product the route of world trade was named – exported silk as a 'digestible' material, one that would not disturb the ecosystem of the settlements into which it was introduced. It was not an end product that would strip local markets like a plague of locusts; on the contrary, the product held hands with agriculture on one side and trade on the other. Emerging as a piece of textile from the hands of its fabricator, it radiated a fertile meaning of consensual dealings. That meaning attaches, too, to all the local craft products of our Syrian heritage. The example of the window frame is only one instance of a pattern of respect through trade that once formed a network through the city.

Um Sa'id, for some time, served as my tailor. She lived in old Homs, was displaced during the war, then got back into her partly destroyed house in the midst of endless mounds of rubble. Her residence is on the second floor of a divided old Islamic house, originally built in the Homsi vernacular of black basalt and white limestone. The portion Um Sa'id and her family had of the property as an inheritance overlooks the other half around the courtyard, where her brother-in-law lives with his family. Other sections of the house belong to other brothers and sisters, each overriding what was originally exposed as a patio or a porch, in order to make the most of the space. The new additions are made from cinder blocks and metal stairs so as to squeeze as much as possible into the spatial maze. No neighbours live in the houses adjoining Um

Sa'id's property: most of them wish to sell to an investor with the financial capacity to build a high-rise in place of the centuries-old house. Um Sa'id has restored her section by installing shabby aluminium-frame windows that leak, curtain walls that vibrate and pressed board doors that don't close properly.

Looking closely, I saw no traces in the other section of the old basalt house. The courtyard next door, where a lemon tree still bears fruit after six years of neglect and where Um Sa'id's husband has put some hens, belongs to neighbours who migrated. 'Your house is built differently; how come?' I ask. Um Sa'id tells me that her mother-in-law wanted a 'modern house' so badly that she threatened to ask for a divorce if her husband didn't oblige. To please his dreamy wife, the husband knocked the old one down and built a 'block' in its place. 'Do you like this one better, or the old one?' I ask again. Um Sa'id confirms to me with certainty that 'everything new is better than the old'. She discreetly mocks my admiring enquiries about the price of the neighbours' vacant house, and explains my 'weird' attitude to her puzzled husband as being characteristic of 'an architect who has a "thing" for old buildings'.

The speculated price of property in destroyed old Homs is no less than 400 USD per square metre. These prices should be considered in light of the fact that the houses are located in a ghost area with no infrastructure, and that due to the war each represents a highly complicated case of unresolved rights between unregistered inheritances, missing owners, multiple ownerships with different narratives that in many cases involve unconfirmed dead or fugitive convicts.

However, people still attach those prices to their properties because they are addicted to the brokering game that they used to play before the war. They still believe that reconstruction will not only compensate them for their losses, but also finally prove to be the worthwhile 'investment' that changes their lives. Hence a city more than half destroyed, like Homs, still hasn't moved a stone from its levelled buildings. Like the window frame, those buildings have fallen victim to the collapse of the fertile cycle under pressure from the Factory.

Um Sa'id's attitude might shock architectural conservatives, but that is not her fault. It is the consequence of false expectations on the part of so-called experts who demand the mummification of 'heritage', without acknowledging that it has been cut out from the cycle on which its life depended and has therefore lost its inner meaning. There is no point in preserving old buildings, as they do in European city centres, only for them to be sold as trophies to the global elite.

Money is the trendsetter; it has always been this way. All houses try to look like those of the rich. We would be naive to forget that style is born in the courts of palaces and the terraces of villas, not the backyards of sheds. When I visited Finland, my host pointed out to me the first stone house around the public square. He told me that before that, local houses had mostly been built of wood; only the well-off built their houses in stone. The most enjoyable part of this story for me was learning that those who couldn't afford to build in stone, painted patterns of stone onto their wooden façades.

But all of these realities are ignored in Alexander's and Scruton's arguments, just as in the recent calls to 'learn lessons' from slums. In an article published in the *Guardian*, Tim Smedley writes: 'We should not romanticize slums, but informal settlements can teach us a lot about society and the economy of resources.'[20] He makes the case that the survival mode under which slums operate offers valuable insights from which city authorities and policymakers can learn. In his point of view, by using 'scarcity as a resource',[21] slums function organically, sustainably and cohesively. The article compares the strength of the slum to the idea of the Wiki City and the Wiki House, which enable people to self-build their habitats using open-source knowledge that architects are encouraged to provide to them.

One is reminded of the award-winning, half-built housing project designed by Pritzker-winning Chilean architect Alejandro

Aravena. We might salute the good intentions of anyone who tries devising an 'architecture for the poor', but we cannot help noticing how ugly the housing has turned out to be after being completed by its inhabitants. People only choose architecture for the poor when they do not have a better option. Providing an empty structure, or an infrastructure framework for people to fill, is doomed to failure without the support of real architectural knowledge.

Some might respond that people in the past routinely built their own housing without much help from professional architects. But that is only part of the story. In the past people had access, not to open-source architecture, but rather to a network of artisanal craftsmen that was also connected with architects. Those who had collaborated with architects consequently developed techniques and products that could be adjusted to suit individual tastes and budgets.

In order to make a difference on a large scale, however, architects need more than just craftsmen on their side. They need to serve as the connecting link between authority and money. Things go wrong when the relationship becomes polar, with money forming one of the poles – money and authority alone, or money and architects alone.

In the best-case scenario, the process goes like this: Authority makes the way. Architects offer solutions. Money creates action, but one must not forget that by its nature, money is interested in making more money, and authority is interested in establishing a name. Sometimes the two exchange interests; so money seeks authority and authority seeks money. Only architects can reconcile these aspirations while accommodating moral messages, social concerns and artistic constraints. But in the rurban world of the Factory, things can get too nebulous for this to be achievable.

The Dutch 'starchitect' Bjarke Ingels recently sent shock waves through advocates of climate and indigenous groups' rights by meeting with the far-right Brazilian president Jair Bolsonaro about tourism and development opportunities in Brazil – a typical Factory City business. In his defence, Ingels has maintained the pragmatic spirit of a businessman by urging detractors not to create a rigid binary between clients who are good or bad; and instead to try offering sustainable alternatives even to those we might disagree with, if it means they might listen. And of course, creating channels for dialogue within the triangle of design, money, and authority is key. But when an architect like Ingels wants to send a message to a president like Bolsonaro, to what exactly does he wish him to 'listen'?

Ingels, who speaks about what he calls 'hedonistic sustainability', also uses the term 'architectural ecosystem' in order to indicate a wider role for architecture. But BIG (Bjarke Ingles Group) wants to design *big*: in proposing his super-ambitious Floating Habitat, he has said he wants to design the world! This proposal involves floating artificial islands, presented as a future habitat for the world's increasing population. Measures of generating and recycling energy are the basic design principle; but what about settlement? What about means of production – who pays for the megastructures, and what kind of business do they perform?

The answer is a mixture of visions that includes elements of Howard's Garden City and Le Corbusier's Machine for Living: in short, a big floating Factory, prefabricated as an embodiment of the five fears, for nomadic tribes to come and fill and unfill. If Ibn Khaldoun could draw any conclusion from the Floating Habitat, it would be that we are back to square one in human civilization.

Great architects are those who have the talent to manage the balancing act between the practical world of networking, money and authority and the creative process of responsible design. The prolific 20th-century Finnish architect Alvar Aalto was a figure who came very close to accomplishing this. Anyone who has seen his work can understand that Aalto managed to form special local understandings with both political authority and economic power, in a variety of contexts.

Aalto's famous creations in the world of wooden furniture were made possible by his longstanding collaboration with Otto

Korhonen, director of one of Finland's most prominent carpentry workshops. Benefiting from Korhonen's deep experience of working with Finnish birch, the curves and bends of Aalto's dream-designs became a mass product. But he was also commissioned extensively on key projects that characterized Finland as an independent nation. These varied widely in scale and Aalto was engaged with aspects from the planning stages to the furnishing, which is only possible with the support of both money and authority.

When I visited Aalto's studio, the first things to catch my eye were some samples of cladding and panelling used for his buildings. The curved shapes and wave-patterned models, cut into sections to show their sophisticated production techniques, made me wonder – probably out loud – 'Who paid for this high level of experimentation?!' Any practising architect can only imagine the response he or she would receive when proposing such detailing, which would involve adapting a whole line of a machinery merely for the sake of an artistic idea. To clad a whole building with bespoke curved tiling is rarely possible, as reality shows. Holding that sample of tiling in my hand, I remarked to our guide: 'Aalto must have had some unswerving producers on his side!' 'Most certainly,' replied the guide, who confirmed that the tiles had been produced through Aalto's established network of industrialists and with the support of politicians.

The Aalto effect was not confined to the prosperous city of Helsinki. He was also commissioned to plan part of the Finnish countryside, so as to mark the shift from the rural and urban Finland of the past to the rurban-agrarian Finland of his day. His commission for the Kokemäenjoki River Valley Regional Plan was again part of his collaboration with an array of decision-makers and facilitators.[22]

The plan of the Kokemäenjoki River Valley was a political decision as much as it was an economic target. Coming out of an expensive war, Finland was facing enormous challenges, including a housing shortage, at a time when regional planning was the order of the day. The ideas of figures like Geddes and Howard were catching on internationally; American models such as Galpin's study or the Tennessee Valley Authority were leading the way for the world to recruit its escaping rural workers into the Factory queue.

Despite being influenced by global trends, Aalto had a high regard for the ethos of organic architecture as a socially responsible tool. He did not cut and paste models from Howard's Garden City or Geddes's conurbation. Instead, for the housing in the Kokemäenjoki River plan, he used as a starting point the traditional linear Finnish village and aimed to confine the main transportation roads to the riverside area, so as to protect the rest of the landscape from radical transformation.[23]

Despite his good intentions, Aalto's aim to leave room for 'organic' processes to evolve was scrapped. In the sixties, technical planning took over and treated everything as a tabula rasa. Even Aalto's plan for the Kokemäenjoki region came, over time, to operate as a Factory Village.

Collaborations between the Finnish Association of Architects (SAFA) and the country's municipalities became the backbone of the rebuilding project in Finland. Nevertheless – and despite the takeover of the Factory in Finland, as has happened everywhere else – the country is increasingly making headlines as a 'rising star' nation. It was ranked in 2019 for the second year in a row as the 'happiest country in the world', offering the best in education and creative innovation in social housing, design and planning.[24] Clearly, this part of the world (which falls in Ibn Khaldoun's seventh region, seemingly isolated in the Nordic ice and darkness) has something to share with the rest of the urbanized world in demonstrating that 'umran may thrive even in challenging natural conditions.

Helsinki brands itself as a 'Design City' that celebrates the legacy of Aalto. My visit there took place in autumn, although it seemed to me like winter, with icy squalls and long heavy showers interrupted occasionally by shy glimmers of pale sunlight. Winter, I was told, is when buses are able to make their journeys among the islands *on* the sea.

The dominant influence of planning and architecture on the city was evident at first sight. Tram lines make their way between lines of equally spaced trees with parallel car streets on either side; façade details of stone, red brick and natural Finnish granite reveal a history of architectural styles including art nouveau, classical revival, and brutalist. The centre of the city is exquisitely opulent. Banks and department stores, many built around the turn of the 20th century, reveal the wealth of their original builders with brass balustrades, elaborate window glazing and metal railings.

Amid the city centre's buzz, surrounded by signs of the cultural identity that Finland has built for itself, I came across a contemporary architectural statement: a housing unit in the size of a single-car parking space rising to three levels, made of wood, free-standing in the middle of a shopping area. Visitors were invited to climb up the narrow stairs, on which you had to angle your shoulders to fit in. This tiny box for living was made a little bit more appealing by Finnish furniture design and the lightness of the wood. The statement was a protest against homelessness: 'It doesn't take more than one parking space' in order to fit a single house in the streets that had become beds for the homeless. This painful truth was apparent under the fluorescent light of closed buildings, where sleeping bags wrapped the crouched bodies of their inhabitants. Further away from the centre, we encountered a greater austerity of design: bland modern and rough brutalist boxes that give louder voice to that architectural protest that is whispered in the centre.

With its hot sauna terrace in front of the Baltic Sea and its public library topped with an entertainment centre, the contrasts of Helsinki confuse you. It occupies a place somewhere between a typical consumer-driven market and a place of all-embracing social ideals. Its central streets have lost their trees and the balconies are void of vegetation, even though the city is surrounded by forests.

It confuses your bearings too, being shredded by a grid plan that criss-crosses the twists and turns of its more topology-friendly older plan, which had a natural division between what ran parallel to the water and what ran towards it.

I tried to get a sense of the city before I read about its architectural history, and more than in any other place I have visited, I was aware of the invisible hand of the architect. Details like the placement of statues, the carving of parks out of the general space and the theatrical exposure of buildings at a corner here or a crossroads there – all such things had a deliberate character of a kind only an architect could have shaped. My first impression was confirmed when I visited the Architecture Museum, where Elina Standertskjold's exhibition 'Arkkitehtuurimme vuosikymmenet' ('Our Architecture through the Decades') was on display. This exhibition told the story of how the city was planned, how its housing was developed and how its style was created over the last two centuries, as Finland evolved from a Grand Duchy of the Russian Empire to a young, independent European nation. Reading its condensed account of history in relation to architecture not only resolved for me some of Finland's many contradictions – it also made me realize that the Finnish experience encapsulates many of the issues relating to globalization and the industrial era that affect the wider world, and that this book has discussed.

Standertskjold explains that between 1860 and 1900 all of Europe was witnessing major social change following the industrial revolution, which had brought railways, steam ships and, for Finland, ice scrapers.[25] This marked the beginning of rural migration to the cities. In what was regarded as a golden age of Finnish art, the first emergence of national character was in a context of passionate nationalism. Finnish building practices adopted idealized styles from the past in a trend termed National Romanticism, or Romantic Idealization. It was accompanied by a proclivity for exhibiting the accomplishments of wealth and industrial advancement on the stone panelling of façades and raised storeys, on the model of market halls.

At this stage, building and expansion were undertaken with little regard for their negative consequences, which included the overcrowding of cities and the breakout of disease. This, we know, was the case in many old European cities as they cleared out the damp, dark, dirty, dense old city to make way for its pneumatic, lofty, liberating replacement. In fact, it parallels the history of modernization all around the world: this was the stage of marching from the village into the city.

The First World War was the final blow to Europe's precarious social structures. Finland experienced civil war and severe food shortages in 1918, and the gap between rich and poor widened. As transportation networks became established the city was allowed to sprawl; and, just as in the final days of the Ottoman Empire, the car industry dictated its market based on pre-assigned supply rather than on demand. The romantic city with its narrow streets wasn't well suited to cars, so it had to be superseded by a modern version tailored to Factory specifications.

All talk of a Finnish national style had faded away. In its place came an eclectic mixture of baroque, rococo and classical façades. Key buildings such as town halls and train stations were entrusted to the architect Eliel Saarinen, whose signature works are celebrated in Finland until this day. Models of housing were changing; urban areas suffered great shortages in housing for the working class. Roughly three-quarters of the rented apartments in Helsinki were merely small boxes comprising a single room, and these housed more than half of the population, resulting in high risks to social stability and health. In response, architects delivered the 'Great Courtyard Block', a Nordic model comprising a core-voided rectangular building with apartments occupying a thin strip around the inner courtyard. Another popular model was the terraced house. Both were designed along simple lines with minimal embellishment apart from their façades, which might be adorned with classical elements. In this way the period of marching led to that of replacement, as the old division between rural and urban gave way to the new rurban ideal.

All of these changes were reinforced during the 1920s. After Finland's civil war, the right gained power – as it often does in times of fear, when the restoration of a lost identity becomes an important card to play. Many Finnish cities and villages were transformed into Factory Cities and Factory Villages: architects were assigned to plan city centres and create new towns connected with highways; the housing crisis worsened as migration from the countryside into urban areas continued. Like the Tower in *The Incredible Tide*, the Factory had plugged its giant sensors into the veins of both city and village. Identity continued to put up a struggle, adopting modernized classical columns from the West or Egyptian motifs from the East. Class differences sharpened even further, with the rich acquiring second homes in the forest while less fortunate people were sold multifunctional open single spaces.

Finland's characteristically dissonant combination of capitalism and socialism was reflected in the government's intervention to lift the country from recession following the Wall Street crash of 1929. In the 1930s the active role of government was quite impressive, achieving land reclamation and establishing wood-processing factories. On the other hand, the wheels of the Factory City were in full motion, leaving nothing untouched. Housing was pushed to the fringes of the city; prefabricated construction was undertaken on a large scale. Tower blocks were isolated from each other by spaces large enough to take the cranes that constructed them. There was no longer a need for decorative motifs, pitched roofs, exterior cladding or framed windows; under the cloak of hygienic living and the war on tuberculosis, the new style became one of quarantine living. This was the stage of exodus from the city to the periphery.

The following four decades continued along the same track. Regional planning of the 1940s focused on profiting from the Factory

Village, which in Finland meant the marketing of harvested forest wood to the building industry along with major plans for the river valleys. The Fifties too witnessed the expansion of the commercial centres that pushed the Finnish people into what were termed the Forest Suburbs. Finnish architects are credited in Standertskjold's notes for attempting to break with the monotony of previous decades by playing with cladding materials and techniques, or varying building heights. Aalto's star began to shine in the early fifties, and Finnish architecture acquired a global reputation for sensitivity towards natural materials expressed with creativity and simplicity.

The sixties saw the rise of the left in response to the social changes that accompanied the shift of Finland from an agricultural nation to an industrial one. Earlier chapters have already discussed how 'umran, the process of human settlement, is fundamentally rooted in agriculture and trade, and how social structures absorb meaning by cultivating those crafts. The industrial age had no limits to its scale, because it wasn't interested in servicing those two crafts and consequently was not in the business of serving human-kind – instead, it subjected humankind to its service.

In short, the Finnish narrative traces a pattern that has been replicated all over the world. The special variations in its story resemble Jane Jacobs's 'windbreakers' in her eye-opening account of 'self-destructive replication'; those Finnish windbreakers are still worthy of acknowledgment, but in spite of them the Finnish family unit of the sixties had collapsed under the pressure of the Factory, just as in so many other countries.

Protests, unions and activism in that decade tried to counter-act the symptoms. Conservation of what little remained succeeded in certain cases, such as in the neighbourhood of Puu-Kapyla in Helsinki; and so did the increased density of the suburbs through grid planning. People also criticized the phenomenon of the starchitect and the excessive emphasis on individualism that had prevailed in the previous decade. Many housing projects were built, creating dormitory suburbs whose inhabitants leave in the morning and return at night.

The left as much as the right has failed to fill the gaps that eroded the structures of society, because it equally failed to address the root of the problem. Therefore the decade of the seventies, and all the decades since, exhibit the same symptoms: exodus, deepening division, more Factory products. Just as in the late Ottoman Empire, Finland began leaning on credit to keep up with the vicious cycle of demand and supply. The successful industry of interior design led to an improvement in living standards, although this only supported the movement towards a consumer society.

Interestingly, though, Standertskjold shows that throughout these decades, Finland at every new juncture would build schools, theatres, and churches. These buildings would change in style and follow the different trends in building materials, riding the same rollercoaster as the rest of the country. But it is worth noting this laudable effort to protect *meaning* by directing energy towards education, culture and religion, which together contain the *raison d'être* of society as a whole. Perhaps this willingness to prioritize meaning is part of the explanation for the success Finland currently enjoys – however, the fact that Helsinki seems to be on the slippery slope towards 'self-destructive repetition' suggests that its success may not continue indefinitely.

Helsinki has recently issued a plan for 'Helsinki Network City 2050',[26] elements of which reflect a Europe-wide shift towards the handing over of regional planning responsibility to the private sector. The specific goals it sets out for 2050 include replacing highways with boulevards; suburbs, big shopping malls and isolating megastructures will also be abandoned. In their place will come green spaces in the shape of intervening 'fingers', multiple centres, and urban structures that fill up the voids. Private car use will be discouraged, with fewer parking spaces and longer routes in order to encourage walking, cycling and public transport, the infrastructure of which will be enhanced.

These objectives sound promising at first sight. But reading the history of planning, as this book has tried to do, and assessing the plan in the context of boundaries and the five fears, makes it apparent that its execution depends solely on the Factory. As in previous attempts at regional planning, the assumption is that the multiple centres are equal and diffused and that all people want basically the same things. There is no acknowledgment of difference equivalent to Galpin's exploration of the rural mindset, or Ibn Khaldoun's of the nomad spirit.

It is true that people in Syria, and those who live in regions of conflict, live at present in greater danger and destitution than those in Europe and other Western countries – although at the time of writing, all are under threat from the Covid-19 pandemic, which plays on the five fears and has a number of effects similar to those of war. Yet even leaving that threat aside, there are some alarming similarities between conflict zones and areas of peace.

What I see in Europe is growing numbers of people rejected by their cities, deprived of their rights, just like us – living on the crumbs of the Factory. If this seems too much like a sweeping generalization, I ask you: why do European (and American) cities fail to contain homelessness? Why are suicide rates increasing? Why have old cities turned into touristic Disneylands? Why do farmers struggle to hold onto their lands, and feel under threat by big agribusiness? Why do indigenous groups still have to fight for basic rights? Why do homes have to be paid out through backbreaking mortgages? Why do educational and health systems feature in every election campaign? Why do people have to pay high rates of tax? And above all, why do people feel cornered in their living space, always shoved forward and away, away from home? If there are oases of hope that still manage to escape the shadow of the giant, in this equation they are negligible.

When people from the West say to me, 'We must help, because we have too much and you have too little,' I'm perplexed, because the truth is that none of us truly has anything; everything belongs to the Factory. Our countries, which were colonized by the West, had their wealth sucked directly into Western factories, but that wealth has never been distributed among the people. All the prosperity that resulted from colonization or was generated in its wake, and that built the European centres in their heydays, is being sold today to global businessmen who have become the actual owners of the cities. The majority of people cannot afford to live in any major city. Students cannot live near colleges, employees cannot live near workplaces, traders cannot afford to open shops in the city, farmers cannot afford to farm their lands. Social housing is a tranquilizer that only leads back to despair, either because it is designed to be 'affordable' – meaning it is too miserable to be inhabited – or because it is sold off to private contractors for renovation and upgrading, adding an extra cost that existing tenants cannot afford. Governments sometimes even hand such projects directly to developers in the first place, so that they are becoming the main providers of housing around the world.

Like scattered tribes of nomads, people today are forced at an unprecedented rate to pack their bags and move further and further from what they might call home. They must think long and hard before starting a family, simply because this requires additional space. That would mean moving away from the city, longer distances to cover between home and work, the school run twice a day and a life of enslavement to pay the bills. They leave the jobs they like doing, which might *mean* something to them, and look for jobs in the Factory that can pay the rent or the mortgage.

The old parts of European towns are meaninglessly 'preserved' and upgraded, partly for the benefit of the wealthy and their international offices, and partly to attract tourists with expensive hotels and restaurants. Sometimes a derelict part of an old town or a run-down city neighbourhood becomes fashionable among artists and young designers, and is briefly re-energized – until it becomes *too* fashionable and attracts the attention of developers, who transfer it into the hands of a wealthier class.

Europe's rich tend to abandon the whole mess for countryside getaways or gated condos, remaining there by night and travelling to the city centre by day. The merging effect of the rurban idea has meant that the vast, kicked-around majority cannot stay too close, nor can they move too far from the city. Near airports, ports and production centres, company headquarters eat up space as well. The countryside is turned into zones for the residences of CEOs who might visit for a day or two every six months. Such companies like to be 'on top of things', so take the prime locations nearest to the action, seizing the space for too many offices, too many facilities and too many vacant residences that become no-go areas at all the crucial business nodes.

The main problem with the way we build today is not just a question of style, nor of blind planning. It is not a matter of achieving goals of sustainability, nor it is about renewable energy. And it is not related to the quantity of what we build; nor is it exactly about the quality either. The problem is that architecture has abandoned its sacrosanct task of promoting 'umran. Almost everything we build is characterized by a separation between man and vocation, between man and nature – and the more we build this way, the deeper the rift gets. Agriculture and trade are turning into a distant mirage in the desert of the Factory: a desert in which most people are forced to become nomads, striving aimlessly to find a home.

We have built ourselves a world of injustice – of Towers and Slums, away from the Land of Hope. But we cannot fight injustice by celebrating slums in formerly colonized countries, or building social housing in colonizer countries. Both are sterile environments in which the five fears dominate: the fear of death in architecture designed specifically for the poor, producing results no one would wish to live in for generations; the fear of need in the lack of abundance and prohibitive meanness; the fear of treachery in our architecture's spatial order and inhuman design; the fear of loneliness in its isolation; and the fear of boredom in the complete loss of meaning. These fears exist at every human scale and intimidating proportions offer no generosity and no exit, denying people acceptance and distracting them from a 'moment of vision'. The old balance between the sublime and the beautiful that works of architecture used to offer has been lost.

We have taken the responsibility of building on the earth so lightly. What Heidegger called 'dwelling', Ibn Khaldoun called 'umran. But both mean building with stability, with prosperity, and with peace. We have seen that we need all three types of 'umran: the nomadic, the rural and the urban. All of these depend on protecting people's rights so that the strong cannot trample the weak – preventing the causes of antagonism, and establishing conditions in which people can offer one another compassion.

The Arabic verb yoemer has various senses, depending on context: to build, to have a long life, to flourish. It generates the significant words imar, the action of building, and 'umran, the end result. However, Arabic also offers a different term for building in its abstract form: yabni, giving us the noun binaa (building). In the Quran, man's mission on earth is to yoemer: not merely to build, but to do so in a way that creates prosperity, justice and peace.

That's why imar demands stability and settlement (in Arabic, istekrar). So although stability and settlement imply stillness – the opposite of movement – yet this stillness is only required for the psyche. It is the kind of stability that encourages us to stay put, to take root where we are in order to initiate the movement required for life and prosperity. In that sense, stability is felt, and movement is built.

My goal in this book has been to show that, like imar, istekrar requires certain conditions: accomplishment, safety and security, and familiarity. These conditions are rooted in a cognitive process that is affected by the surrounding built environment. The 'five fears' reflect key elements of this process, and each fear drives the individual into a searching journey:

- The fear of death leads to the search for continuation (*accomplishment*).

- The fear of need leads to the search for abundance (*safety and security*).

- The fear of treachery leads to the search for boundaries (*safety and security*).

- The fear of loneliness leads to the search for acceptance (*safety and security*).

- The fear of boredom leads to the search for meaning (*familiarity*).

Each of these journeys has a tipping point at which balance is lost. When this occurs, rights are damaged, antagonism rises and compassion disappears. Eventually, movement stops. Life stops. We lose *imar* and we lose *istekrar*, both of which are needed for us to call a place home. Each is a precondition of the other, and each affects the other: they make a cycle, a cycle that is damaged when *imar* is lost and also when *istekrar* is undermined.

I believe that the damage can be reversed by means of tried and tested approaches such as the system of *miri* lands, the neighbourhoods of the forty occupations, and the *waqf* system. These were strategies that once successfully prevented the kind of problems we grapple with today.

If the scale of the task seems overwhelming, there are plenty of little places that we can start from: fighting real-estate business where possible by means of taxes, legislation and by personal self-control. Avoiding credit in the same frame of work, in combination with compensating measures such as supporting local production, agriculture and small trade. We can differentiate between good and bad business (or, to use the terms of this book, Factory business) by looking at the nature of production and questioning how and why it is undertaken.

Paying attention to these nuances can make a huge difference. Businesses whose motives are benign need no self-promotion, as they are a necessary part of the life cycle. Agriculture and trade work in this way: they do not drive people far and out, they bring them together and in. Modern nomadism is a way of life that should neither be condemned nor enforced, but it's a choice that should be controlled, while bearing in mind that – on a large scale – it is the least productive form of human settlement, incapable of building a civilization. It is a phenomenon that most of our modern world suffers from, and we cannot overlook it. A balance between the three types of 'umran is what we should aspire to.

The layers of built history in Damascus, where the stranger used to sleep standing on his shadow – where the *waqf*, the *miris* and the 'forties' hugged the minarets and the people below, bloomed with lemons and jasmine, and yielded books, silk and golden wheat – tell us that the Land of Hope is achievable. But we need to find a way of reaching it before the Tide.

NOTES

CHAPTER 1

1　Lindemann Dehousing Memorandum, 30 March 1942. Quoted at https://en.wikipedia. org/wiki/Dehousing#Production_ and_contents_of_the_dehousing_ paper.

2　Peter Frankopan, *The Silk Roads: A New History of the World* (Vintage Books, 2015), p. 13.

3　Edmund Burke, *A Philosophical Enquiry into the Sublime and Beautiful* (Oxford University Press, 2015), p. 51.

4　Frank Lloyd Wright, 'In the Cause of Architecture, VI: The Meaning of Materials – Glass' (July 1928), https://www.architecturalrecord. com/articles/11508-in-the-cause- of-architecture-vi-the-meaning- of-materialsglass?page=2&v= preview.

5　Ibid.

6　Quoted in 'Why "Deaths of Despair" May Be a Warning Sign for America – Moving Upstream', *Wall Street Journal* (27 February 2018), https://www. wsj.com/articles/why-deaths- of-despair-may-be-a-warning- sign-for-america-moving- upstream-1519743601.

7　See for example http://alwaght. com/en/News/70585/Constructive- Chaos-Theory-When-Terrorism-is- of-Much-Avail-to-US.

8　Adolf Hitler, *Hitler's Table Talk, 1941–1944, His Private Conversations*, trs Norman Cameron and R. H. Stevens (New York: Enigma Books, 2000), p. 202; see https:// en.wikipedia.org/wiki/Balance_ of_power_(international_ relations)#cite_note-24.

9　A. J. P. Taylor, *The Struggle for Mastery in Europe* (Oxford University Press, 1954), p. xix; see https://en.wikipedia.org/wiki/ Balance_of_power_(international_ relations)#cite_note-10.

10　'character, n.', *OED Online*, oed. com.

11　*1986 Technical Review Summary. Restoration of Khan Asaad Pasha, Damascus, Syria*, https://s3.us- east-1.amazonaws.com/media. archnet.org/system/publications/ contents/726/original/FLS0736. pdf?1384748534.

12　My translation; see http:// damascus-friends.com/modules/ printArticle.php?nb=54 (Arabic).

13　Frank Lloyd Wright, 'In the Cause of Architecture, III: The Meaning of Materials – Stone' (July 1928), https://www.architecturalrecord. com/articles/11510-in-the-cause- of-architecture-iii-the-meaning- of-materialsstone?page=2.

14　Ibid.

15　Ibid.

16　Ibid.

17　Alain de Botton, *The Architecture of Happiness* (Penguin Books, 2006), p. 210.

CHAPTER 2

1 Timur Zolotoev, 'Rem Koolhaas: "Beauty can give you a false sense of existential security"', *Strelka* (24 July 2018), https://strelkamag.com/en/article/rem-koolhaas-vladimir-pozner.

2 Freud's essay 'On Transience' (1916), quoted in de Botton, *The Architecture of Happiness*, p. 15.

3 Ibid., p.16.

4 Eduardo Porter, 'Why Big Cities Thrive, and Smaller Ones Are Being Left Behind' (10 October 2017), https://www.nytimes.com/2017/10/10/business/economy/big-cities.html.

5 Ibid.

6 Ibid.

7 Peter Frankopan, *The Silk Roads: A New History of the World* (Vintage Books, 2015), p. 60.

8 Munir Al-Khouri Issa As'ad, *History of Homs: Vol. 2*, Arabic Edition (Publications of the Archbishopric of Roman Orthodox of Homs, 1984), p. 360.

9 Ibid.

10 Nuhad Samaan, public lecture, Homs, 2016.

11 See Jane Jacobs, *The Death and Life of Great American Cities* (Random House, 1961).

12 Ibid., p. 243.

13 Ibid.

14 See Nuhad Samaan, *From Diaries of the Archbishop of Homs of Roman Orthodox: Athnasius Ataallah 1888–1891* (Publications of The Archbishopric of Roman Orthodox of Homs, n.d.), p. 20.

15 Jacobs, *The Death and Life of Great American Cities*, p. 255.

16 Frankopan, *The Silk Roads*, pp. 5, 7. Much of the information I refer to in the following paragraph is discussed in detail in this book; see pp. 11, 46–7, 48, 49.

17 Ibn Khaldoun, *The Introduction: vol. I* (Dar Yaarob, 2004), p. 246. All English translations of excerpts from this title are my own.

18 Ibid., p. 287.

19 Nuhad Samaan, public lecture, Homs, 2016.

20 Ibid.

21 'Wolf Reintroduction Changes Ecosystem in Yellowstone', (January 2019), https://www.yellowstonepark.com/things-to-do/wolf-reintroduction-changes-ecosystem.

22 Ibn Khaldoun, *The Introduction: vol. I*, p. 278.

23 Al-Bir charity website, http://al-birr.org/birr/?page_id=1354.

24 Mark Muro, 'Where the Robots Are', *Brookings* (14 August 2017), https://www.brookings.edu/blog/the-avenue/2017/08/14/where-the-robots-are/.

25 Ibid.

CHAPTER 3

1 Gaston Bachelard, *The Poetics of Space: The Classic Look at How We Experience Intimate Places* (Beacon Press, 1994), p. 15.

2   Ibid., p.16.

3   Ibid., p.17.

4   Ibid.

5   Ibid., p.18.

6   Ibid.

7   Ibid.

8   Ibid., p.20.

9   Ibid.

10 Ibid., p. 17.

11 Alain de Botton, *The Architecture of Happiness* (Penguin Books, 2006), p. 245.

12 Ibid. p., 246.

13 Ibid. p., 247.

14 Kevin Lynch, *The Image of the City* (MIT Press, 1960), p. 62.

15 Ibid.

16 Ibid., p. 65.

17 Lynch, *The Image of the City*, p. 100.

18 Jane Jacobs, *The Death and Life of Great American Cities* (Random House, 1961), p. 268.

19 Ibid., pp. 268–9.

20 Roger Scruton, 'Aesthetic Education and Design', conference lecture, Architecture and Philosophy (University of Bamberg, 2016).

21 Farhan Samanani, 'Common Ground', *Aeon* (6 July 2017), https://aeon.co/essays/whats-the-best-way-to-find-common-ground-in-public-spaces.

22 Ibid.

23 Linda Schatkowski Schilcher, *Families in Politics: Damascene Factions and Estates of the 18th and 19th Centuries* (Dar al-Jumhurya, 1998), p. 33.

24 Ibid.

25 'The English are determined to sustain the Turkish Government, and to sustain the Druses, however much it may deplore the enormities perpetrated by them. Its policy requires that this empire shall remain in the hands of a weak Government, in order that the British possessions in India may not be imperilled. France and Russia would be willing to see the country divided. Austria has but little influence, and the policy of our American Consul is to protect all citizens, and to avoid all interference in the politics of the country other than that dictated by humanity for the relief of the starving and persecuted Christians' – from 'The Civil War in Syria: Interesting Documentary Evidence Condition of the American Mission', *New York Times* (18 July 1860), http://www.nytimes.com/1860/07/18/news/civil-war-syria-interesting-documentary-evidence-condition-american-mission.html?pagewanted=2.

26 'Correspondence of the London Times. ALEXANDRIA, Monday, June 25, 1860. "The French mail steamer from Syria, which arrived here yesterday, has brought us full and recent particulars of the savage internecine warfare raging between the Druses and Maronite Christians of Mount Lebanon.

We had previously heard that the dissensions between the two rival tribes had at the latter end of last month broken out into actual hostilities; villages had been attacked and burnt down, and in many the silk crop of cocoons, the principal source of subsistence of the inhabitants, had been utterly destroyed, but the loss of life was not great"' – from 'The Civil War in Syria', *New York Times* (21 July 1860), http://www. nytimes.com/1860/07/21/news/ the-civil-war-in-syria.html.

27 Schilcher, *Families in Politics*, p. 96.

28 Jonathan Sperber, *Europe 1850–1914*, 'Part 2: The age of uncertainty, 1871–1895' (Routledge, 2009). Recessions in years: 1847, 1857–8, 1870, 1873–9, 1882–6).

29 See Schilcher, *Families in Politics*.

30 Ibid.

31 'The Paris correspondent of the Daily News, writing on Thursday evening, says: "The Presse states that the Sultan's letter will not prevent the sending of a French expedition to Syria in concert with the other Powers, and without any opposition from the Porte, and all the Government journals continue in very strong language to urge the necessity of intervention without loss of time. I have, however, reason to believe that these papers are traveling much faster than diplomacy;

and that, although the French Government desires to land troops in Syria, and is making ready to do so, it has as yet taken no final resolution on the subject, and that negotiations with other Powers, and particularly with England, are still going on"' – from 'The Syrian Massacres: A French Expedition', *New York Times* (3 August 1860), http://www. nytimes.com/1860/08/03/news/ the-syrian-massacres-a-french-expedition.html.

32 'The Mercantile Courier, of Genoa, publishes an authentic account of the massacre at Damascus up to the 10th of July, inclusive, 3,000 Christians had taken refuge in the citadel occupied by the Algerines under ABDEL KADER. The town was in the power of the murderers and incendiaries to the number of 24,000, principally Druses and Bedouins. The Turkish garrison consisted of 5,000 men, who were inactive or hostile' – from 'The Syrian Outbreak: Details Of The Damascus Massacre. Foreign Intervention In Syria', *New York Times* (3 August 1860), http:// www.nytimes.com/1860/08/13/ news/syrian-outbreak-details-damascus-massacre-foreign-intervention-syria. html?pagewanted=all.

33 Ibn Khaldoun, *The Introduction: vol. I* (Dar Yaarob, 2004), p. 247. All English translations of excerpts

from this title are my own.

34 M. K. Smith, 'What is community?' (2001), *The Encyclopedia of Informal Education*, http://www.infed.org/community/community.htm.

35 Charles Josiah Galpin, *Rural Life* (The Century Co., 1918), p. 36.

36 Ibid., p. 11.

37 Ibid., p. 13.

38 Ibid., p. 42.

39 Ibid.,

40 Ibid., p. 51.

41 Ibid., p. 43.

42 Ibid., p. 45.

CHAPTER 4

1 'The era of industrialization', *Encyclopedia Britannica*, https://www.britannica.com/topic/urban-planning/The-era-of-industrialization#ref292929.

2 Ibn Khaldoun, *The Introduction: vol. I* (Dar Yaarob, 2004), pp. 125–37. All English translations of excerpts from this title are my own.

3 Nuhad Samaan, personal interview, Homs, 2017.

4 Ibid.

5 'Land Code of 1858', *Encyclopedia of the Modern Middle East and North Africa* (Gale, 2004), https://www.encyclopedia.com/humanities/encyclopedias-almanacs-transcripts-and-maps/land-code-1858.

6 Ibid.

7 Nuhad Samaan, personal interview, Homs, 2017.

8 Ibid.

9 'Land Code of 1858', *Encyclopedia of the Modern Middle East and North Africa*.

10 Ibid.

11 Ibid.

12 Much of the detail in this paragraph comes from Nuhad Samaan (personal interview, Homs, 2017).

13 'Land Code of 1858', *Encyclopedia of the Modern Middle East and North Africa*.

14 Nuhad Samaan, personal interview, Homs, 2017.

15 Ibid.

16 Ibid.

17 'Land Code of 1858', *Encyclopedia of the Modern Middle East and North Africa*.

18 Hanna Batatu, *Syria's Peasantry: The Descendants of Its Lesser Rural Notables and Their Politics* (1999), quoted in Laura Cunial, *Briefing Note: Housing, Land and Property in the Syrian Republic* (May 2016), https://www.nrc.no/globalassets/pdf/reports/housing-land-and-property-hlp-in-the-syrian-arab-republic.pdf.

19 Caitlin Werrell and Francesco Femia, 'William Polk: Deep Dive On Syria, Including Drought', *The Center for Climate and Security* (10 December 2013), https://climateandsecurity.org/2013/12/10/william-polk-deep-dive-on-syria-including-drought/.

20 Ibn Khaldoun, *The Introduction:*

vol. I, p. 189.

21 Quoted in Robin Pogrebin, 'Top Architecture Prize Goes to Low-Cost Housing Pioneer From India', *New York Times*, https://www.nytimes.com/2018/03/07/arts/design/pritzker-prize-balkrishna-doshi.html.

22 China's new Silk Road: https://www.weforum.org/agenda/2017/06/china-new-silk-road-explainer/; Russia's green corridor with Damascus (Arabic): https://arabic.rt.com/news/851433-%D9%85%D9%85%D8%B1-%D8%A3%D8%AE%D8%B6%D8%B1-%D8%A8%D9%8A%D9%86-%D9%85%D9%88%D8%B3%D9%83%D9%88-%D9%88%D8%AF%D9%85%D8%B4%D9%82/.

CHAPTER 5

1 Eugene Rogan, *The Great War and Modernity in the Middle East*, recorded talk, The Academy of the Kingdom of Morocco (26 January 2017).

2 See Wendell O'Brien, 'Boredom: A History of Western Philosophical Perspectives', https://iep.utm.edu/page/2/?cat=-%201#H2.

3 Jan Slaby, 'The Other Side of Existence: Heidegger on Boredom' (2010). http://janslaby.com/downloads/slaby_heideggerboredom.pdf.

4 Ibid., p. 9.

5 Ibid., pp. 8–9.

6 Ibid., p. 14.

7 Ibid., p. 17.

8 Ibid., p. 19.

9 A. E. Jeffreys, 'SP/Syria 7340 Assignment Report: Development of the Al Assad National Library', UNESCO Paris (2 May 1984), Serial No. PMH/PGI/oPS/84/2I5(SP), p. 5.

10 Jeffreys, 'Development of the Al Assad National Library'.

11 Ibid.

12 Ibid., p. 4.

13 See http://www.alassad-library.gov.sy/.

14 Hamddo bin Omar, 'Research on Al Zahiriyya Library and Its Scholars As an Exemplar' (published in Arabic; 22 March 2012), http://www.grenc.com/show_article_main.cfm?id=25635.

15 Talal Akili, *The Great Mosque of Damascus: From Roman Temple to Monument of Islam* (Municipal Administration Modernization Program, 2009), p. 14.

16 Christopher Alexander, *The Timeless Way of Building* (Oxford University Press, 1979), p. 238.

17 Roger Scruton, 'The Threat of "Genius" to Truly Successful Architecture', *The American Conservative*, 7 September 2018, https://www.theamericanconservative.com/urbs/the-threat-of-genius-to-truly-successful-architecture/.

18 Alexander, *The Timeless Way of Building*, p. 223.

19 Scruton, 'The Threat of "Genius"'.

20 Tim Smedley, 'Sustainable Urban Design: Lessons to Be Taken from Slums', *The Guardian* (5 June 2013), https://www.theguardian.com/sustainable-business/sustainable-design-lessons-from-slums.

21 Ibid.

22 See *Summary: Architects, War, and the Governance of Social–Spatial Relationships in Localities: A Study of Alvar Aalto's Kokemäenjoki River Valley Regional Plan As a Project of Regulation of Space*, trans. Vesa Raiskila, https://elektra.helsinki.fi/sumnuppo.pdf.

23 Ibid.

24 See https://worldhappiness.report/ed/2019/.

25 Elina Standertskjold, *Arkkitehtuurimme Vuosikymmenet 1900–1920, 1930–1950, 1960–1980* (Rakennustieto Oy, 2011). The information I have discussed here and in the paragraphs that follow was displayed in an exhibition at the Museum of Architecture in Helsinki, September 2017.

26 Ari Hynynen, *From Alvar Aalto to Network City: Reflections from the 1940s Kokemäenjoki Regional Plan*, Tampere University of Technology, Laboratory of Architecture, Seinäjoki Urban Laboratory, The 3rd Alvar Aalto Researchers Network Seminar – *Why Aalto?* 9–10 June 2017, Jyväskylä, Finland.

ACKNOWLEDGMENTS

It feels more solemn than usual to send my work out into a transforming world. Whatever our personal convictions, we can all agree that these are troubled times. Facing such a reality, being a part of this universe, we can only hope to be doing something right. In this spirit I place my work in the hands of readers, with apologies for any errors.

This book owes its existence to many new experiences and sources of inspiration, but also to a lot of kindness and generosity, for all of which I am immensely grateful.

I thank my husband, partner and best friend, Ghassan, and our two precious children, Naya and Ayk, for their unconditional love and support and for lending me their souls and minds without a blink of hesitation. I have benefited from their wisdom and their thoughts more than I can credit. It may not be an exaggeration to say that I had four minds and eight eyes to aid me in writing this book, but I'm mostly grateful for the three great hearts in which I pray I will always be blessed to live.

I also thank my commissioning editor, Lucas Dietrich, for his exceptional work and the efforts he has made to take the book from the realm of chaotic ideas into that of professional publishing. I'm forever indebted to him for the patience, care and respect with which the project was treated, and the extra miles that were taken in order to place a piece of my mind between two covers. None of this would have been possible without Lucas at the helm.

Roger Scruton sadly died before seeing the finished book, but I hope that my gratitude will reach him in a better place. The first draft, which he read, benefited from the last shafts of his great intellect through the invaluable notes and remarks he so generously offered. May his soul rest in peace.

My thanks also go to James Atlee for reading and pointing out errors and contradictions in the early manuscript. Many arguments in the book became more polished thanks to his excellent feedback.

I'm very grateful to my editor, Camilla Rockwood, for the brilliant work she's done on the text, correcting and refining its language and sparing the reader the arduous task of deciphering its more complex meanings.

Two beautiful souls I have not yet had the fortune to meet in person (but will keep hoping to) are Rikki Ducornet and Rick Simonson. Our spirits definitely managed to connect across the oceans. I'm very thankful for their friendship and for the books they sent – despite the great distance separating the US and Syria.

My friends in Damascus, Ahmad Jmaiel and Hanan Hammoud, became a family in times when real families are shattered. Their warm welcome is the warmest, just as their great city is the greatest. Their friendship allowed me to look at my country's capital with fresh eyes, and for that – and much more – I'm forever grateful.

I also felt welcomed by audiences around the world, and cities across the globe. I cannot thank them all enough for inspiring me and embracing me with wide arms, for sparking the most exciting conversations and showering a stranger with sincere affection. I thank with all my heart the many friends I've made on the way in the different cities I've been to, who so kindly welcomed me to their homes and their dinner tables. I find hope in humanity meeting you all, and have found home in your generous hearts.

Page numbers in *italic* refer
to the illustrations

Aalto, Alvar 196–8, 203
Abd Al-Hamid, Sultan
  168, 181
Abd Al-Qadir Al-Jazairei 123
abundance 51–4, 77
Adjaye, David 108, 110–11
Adnan and Lina 32–3
Aesop 125
The Age of Shame (TV series)
  145–6
Agrarian Reformation
  Code (1958) 141–2
agriculture 101, 125–9, 135,
  143, 147, 161–2, 165
Aishti department store,
  Beirut 108, 110–11
Al-Assad, Hafiz 177
Al-Azm, Pasha As'ad 37
Al-Azm family 116–19,
  124, 129
Al-Badyia 137
Al-Bara 57
Al-Bir 87–8
Al-Buzuriyah Souk,
  Damascus 37
Al-Hasaka 137
Al-Meedan, Damascus
  117–18, 124, 129
Al-Zahiriyya Library,
  Damascus 180–2, 182
Aleppo 33, 46, 49, 56, 115,
  136, 183
Alexander, Christopher
  186–90, 194
Algeria 86, 181
allotments 105–6
American Council,
  Istanbul 170–1
Andersen, Hans
  Christian 31
Ankara 189

apartments 76, 94–7, 105,
  167–9, 186, 201–2
Ar-Raqqa 137
Aravena, Alejandro 194–5
architects 188–9, 195–6
Architecture Museum,
  Helsinki 200
Armageddon 43
art galleries 80
As-Suwayda 136
'asabiyya (kinship) 71–2,
  73–4, 77, 117, 118, 124
Assad Library, Damascus
  175–80, 178–9, 182
Assad Pasha 117–18
Assyrians 46
Aswad, Raghib 177
Australia 80–1, 95, 163
Austria 123–4
automation 57–60, 88
Ayyubid dynasty 180

Ba'ath party 31, 86, 142
Bachelard, Gaston 92–6,
  98, 106, 128
Baibars, Zahir 180
Barada, river 150, 151, 177
Bates Smart McCutcheon 81
beauty 51–3
Bedouin 67, 71, 74, 76–7,
  117, 122
Beirut 108–12, 110–11,
  121–2, 184
Bellamy, Edward 131
BIG (Bjarke Ingles Group)
  196
Black Sea 70, 71
Bolsonaro, Jair 195–6
Bombay 167
boredom, fear of 167–210
boundaries 94–5, 98–107
Brazil 195
Bristol 112–14, 113
Britain 85, 119–24, 164, 171

British Library 180
Burj Khalifa, Dubai 25, 26
Burke, Edmund 23, 24
Byzantine Empire 41, 56

Canada 163
cars 55, 97, 170–1, 201, 204–5
Caspian Sea 71
Catholic Church 120–1
Central Asia 70
Chapman Taylor Architects
  158
character 36, 40–1
China 41, 70, 138, 164, 191–2
Christ 43
Christians 42, 43, 53, 72,
  120–1, 122–3
Churchill, Winston 19, 21, 35
class divisions 54, 60, 67, 202
Collins Place, Melbourne
  81, 83
Cologne 19
Colorado 75
computers 57–60
consumers 66, 74–5
continuity 19–49, 51
courtyards 37, 82, 94, 99
Covid-19 pandemic 205
Crac des Chevaliers,
  Homs 46
cyber-sphere 57–60

Damascus 17, 49, 114–18,
  148–9, 159
  Al-Buzuriyah Souk 37
  Al-Meedan 117–18, 124, 129
  Al-Zahiriyya Library 180–2,
    182
  Assad Library 175–80, 178–9,
    182
  book stalls 151–2, 152
  duality 183–6
  earthquake (1757) 36
  foreign interventions 120–3

Great Umayyad Mosque 43, 47, 116, 153–8, 156–7, 161
Green Meadow 85
Hamrawi neighbourhood 153–4
homeless in 175
Khan Al-Azm 36–9, 38, 46, 116
markets 184–5
Marota City 153
Massar Learning Centre 86
real estate market 167, 168
Straight Street 43–6, 44–5, 47
textile industry 67
Damascus Book Fair 182
Damascus Holdings 153
Damascus University 175, 182–3
Daraa 136
Dark Ages 71
Darwish, Mahmoud 114
Dayr Al-Zawr 137
de Botton, Alain 41–2, 97
Dead Cities of Syria 56–7, 58–9, 62–3, 70
death, fear of 19–49, 209
Deaton, Angus 29
Detroit 55–6, 57, 60, 64, 66, 67, 70, 78, 88
Doshi, Balkrishna 161
Dresden 19
drought 143, 147
Druze 119, 121, 122
Dubai 10, 25, 27, 79–80, 150, 167, 170
Dunikowski, Marek 176

Earle, Edward Mead 35
Ecochard, Michel 176–7
edges 98–107
education 162, 204
Egypt 41, 141–2, 147
Eiffel Tower, Paris 26

electricity 57–60
elk 75
Empire State Building, New York 26
ethical trade 106–7
Euphrates, river 136, 137

Factory Syndrome/City 55–70, 73–7, 88–9, 102, 106, 126, 128–9, 134, 146, 170, 188, 202–3, 205
Fertile Crescent 136, 150
feudalism 142
Finland 194, 196–205
Finnish Association of Architects 198
First World War 201
flats 94–5, 96–7
France 85–6, 119–20, 121–4, 141, 171
Frankopan, Peter 20
Franta, Aleksander 176
Freud, Sigmund 52

Galpin, Charles Josiah 126–9, 132, 133, 134, 147, 161, 170, 198, 205
Garden City movement 131–3, 196, 198
Geddes, Patrick 133, 170, 198
generosity 78–84
Ghouta 150–1, 158, 159, 184
glass 23–4
globalization 20, 75
Gothic architecture 41
Great Nouri Mosque, Homs 74
Great Umayyad Mosque, Damascus 43, 47, 116, 153–8, 156–7, 161
Greater Syria 115, 119–22, 135
Greece 41
Green Meadow, Damascus 85

Grenfell Tower, London 97
Guardian 194

Hama 37, 116, 136, 182–3
Hamburg 19
Hamrawi neighbourhood, Damascus 153–4
Hatim Altaaey 76
Heidegger, Martin 171–4, 208
Helsinki 197, 198–201, 203, 204–5
Henning and Larsen 85
heritage 27, 36, 39–40, 42–9, 194
Hisya 140
Hitler, Adolf 35
homelessness 21, 87, 114, 174–5, 199, 205
Homs 27, 56, 67–70, 73–4, 87–8, 105–6, 129, 139, 182–3, 185, 186, 192–4
Crac des Chevaliers 46
Great Nouri Mosque 74
Khaled Ibn Al-Walid Mosque 47
Souk Al-Badou 74
Temple of the Sun 74
Hong Kong 167
Houran 116
houses: Islamic 81–2, 94, 98–9
oneiric 92–3, 94
vernacular rural houses 95
Howard, Ebenezer 131–3, 134, 196, 198
Hume, David 34
hurumat (respect for sacred things) 105

Ibn Khaldoun 71–2, 73, 76, 77, 126, 127, 133, 134, 146, 147–50, 162, 196, 198, 205, 208
Idlib 56, 136

imar 208–9
industrialization 64–5, 95, 127, 133, 170
informalities 144–5, 167–9, 191
Ingels, Bjarke 195–6
inheritance laws 161–4
International Convention 123–4
International Union of Architects 175–6
internet 57–60, 64
Iraq 46, 135, 147
ISIS 42, 49
Islam 53, 72, 73–4
Islamic houses 81–2, 94, 98–9
Islamic law 105, 135, 138, 141, 142, 168
Istanbul 170–1
istekrar (stability) 208–9

Jacobs, Jane 68, 69–70, 77, 99–102, 106, 160, 203
Japan 34
Jeffreys, A. E. 177–80
Jews 120

Kazakhstan 181–2
Key, Alexander 32
Khaled Ibn Al-Walid Mosque, Homs 47
Khan As'ad Pasha Al-Azm, Damascus 36–9, 38, 46, 116
Kharab al-Shams Basilica 62–3
Kierkegaard, Søren 172
Kilburn, London 103–4, 105
kinship ('*asabiyya*) 71–2, 73–4, 77, 117, 118, 124
Kokemäenjoki River Valley Regional Plan 197–8
Koolhaas, Rem 51–3
Korhonen, Otto 196–7

land ownership 132, 135–6, 138–44
Latakia 137
Law No. 10 (2018) 169
Le Corbusier 97, 196
Lebanon 108–12, 119, 120, 122, 124, 162, 169
Letchworth Garden City 132
Levant 42, 115, 119, 122, 135, 136, 150
liberalism 65
Limestone Massif 56–7
Lindemann, Frederick 19, 21, 25
London 97, 103–4, 167
loneliness, fear of 131–65, 209
Lutheranism 53
Lynch, Kevin 99–102, 106

malkhane (grants) 136
Mamluks 180–1
market system 65–7, 74
Maronites 119, 121
Marota City, Damascus 153
Marx, Karl 142
mass production 53, 55, 77, 134, 171
Massar Learning Centre, Damascus 86
Maya 41
Mazurkiewicz, Małgorzata 176
mechanization 57–60
Medhat Pasha 181
Meissner, Jan Jacek 176
Melbourne 80–1, 83, 95, 108
Mesopotamia 135, 150
Miecznikowski, Wojciech 176
Mies van der Rohe, Ludwig 53, 54
migration 67, 95, 125, 126, 143, 144

minimalism 53–4
miri lands 135, 138, 140, 141, 142, 161, 168, 190, 209
Miyazaki, Hayao 32
modernism 54–5
modernity 28–30, 75, 89
money 194–6
Mongolia 70
Moscow 167
Mosul 33
Mount Qasioun, Damascus 178, 191
mulk land 135, 138
murabe'a ('quarterer') 140
Muro, Mark 60–4, 88
Murray, Douglas 158
Muslim Brotherhood 31

Nagasaki 19
Napoleonic Wars 120
National Romanticism 200–1
need, fear of 51–89, 209
New York 26, 97, 167
New York Times 60–4, 122
Nimrud 46
nomads 71–7, 117, 126, 138

oneiric house 92–3, 94
Ottoman Empire 37, 68–9, 74, 94, 115–17, 118–20, 122, 124, 134–6, 137–41, 170–1
Ottoman Land Code (1858) 137–41
Ottoman Land Reclamation Act 136
Oxford 158–60, 159

Palmyra 46
pandemics 174, 205
Paris 17, 167
Pascal, Blaise 172
Pei, I. M. 81
Persia 70–1
Poland 176

postmodernism 54–5
property investment 146,
   153, 163–4, 169, 174
Prussia 123–4
public spaces 104–5
pyramids 25

Qabbani, Nizar 17
Qamishli 137
Quran 208

Radburn, New Jersey 132
raqaba 135
reconstruction 46–9
religion 48, 72–3, 77, 204
rent laws 143–4, 168
Revolution of Keserwan 119
rights 104–5, 134, 161–2
Rilke, Rainer Maria 52
Riyadh 79
robots 88
Rogan, Eugene 170–1
Roman Empire 43, 71
Rome 17, 42, 71
Rotterdam 10
Russia 123–4, 164, 200

Saarinen, Eliel 201
Sa'id (Mamluk ruler) 180
Samaan, Nuhad 74, 136, 137
Samanani, Farhan 103–4, 105
São Paulo 189
Saudi Arabia 79
Sauvaget, Jean 183
Schilcher, Linda
   Schatkowski 115–16, 117,
   121
Schopenhauer, Arthur 172
Scruton, Roger 102, 103, 104,
   107, 187–9, 194
Second World War 9, 19, 35,
   42, 53–4, 64
sectarianism 118–19
security 51–3

segregation 55–6, 60, 102–3
Seneca 172
Serjilla 58–9
Sheikh Al-Kar 151
Sidon 115
Silk Road 70–1, 154, 164
Singapore 167
skyscrapers 97
Slaby, Jan 172
slums 29, 194, 207
Smedley, Tim 194
social breakdown 29
social cohesion 77, 103, 107
Souk Al-Badou, Homs 74
Standertskjold, Elina 200–1,
   203, 204
Straight Street, Damascus
   43–6, 44–5, 47
Sufism 53, 117
Sykes–Picot accord (1916) 34,
   115, 124

Taher Al Jaza'ari, Sheikh 181
Tamerlane 154
Tanzimat 134–5, 141, 142, 143,
   147, 164
Tartous 137, 183
tasaruf rights system 135, 161
tech campus 64–5
television 30–3
Temple of the Sun, Homs 74
Tennessee Valley Authority
   198
Tokyo 10, 167
tourism 42–3, 159, 160, 206
trade 65–7, 70–1, 74, 106–7,
   117–18, 165, 174, 185–6
treachery, fear of 91–129, 209
Tripoli 115
Turkey 168

Um Sa'id 192–4
Umayyad dynasty 66
Umayyad Mosque, Aleppo

46
'umran (urbanization) 71, 77,
   190, 198, 203, 207, 208
UNESCO 56, 175–6, 177
United Arab Republic 141–2
United States 29, 55–6, 61,
   101, 128–9, 131, 164
urban warfare 20, 25
urbanization ('umran) 71, 77,
   190, 198, 203, 207, 208
Ustunkok, Okan 38–9

Venturi, Robert 54–5
Victoria, Queen 151

The Waiting (TV series) 144–5
Wall Street crash (1929) 202
waqf (endowment) 82–7,
   88–9, 138, 154, 168, 180–2,
   189, 209
waterfronts 101
Westgate shopping centre,
   Oxford 158–60, 159
Wiki City 194
Wiki House 194
wolf, gray 75
World Economic Forum on
   the Middle East and North
   Africa (2017) 60
Wright, Frank Lloyd 23–4,
   40–1

Yellowstone National Park
   75
Young Turks 141

For Ghassan

On page 2: Contrasting architecture in the city of Damascus. The luxury Four Seasons Hotel, which currently houses United Nations staff, overlooks the Takiyya Al-Sulaymaniyya Mosque and Hospice. Mount Qasioun can be seen in the background, with the many informal settlements sitting upon it.

First published in the United Kingdom in 2021 by
Thames & Hudson Ltd, 181A High Holborn, London WC1V 7QX

First published in the United States of America 2021 by
Thames & Hudson Inc., 500 Fifth Avenue, New York, New York 10110

Building for Hope © 2021 Thames & Hudson Ltd, London.

Text and illustrations © 2021 Marwa al-Sabouni

British Library Cataloguing-in-Publication Data
A catalogue record for this book is available from the British Library

Library of Congress Control Number 2020940845

ISBN 978-0-500-34372-2

Printed and bound in Slovenia by DZS-Grafik d.o.o.

Be the first to know about our new releases,
exclusive content and author events by visiting
thamesandhudson.com
thamesandhudsonusa.com
thamesandhudson.com.au